FINAL ACCOUNTS
PREPARATION

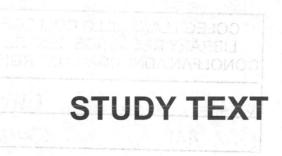

STUDY TEXT

Qualifications and Credit Framework

AQ2016

This Study Text supports study for the following AAT qualifications:

AAT Advanced Diploma in Accounting – Level 3

AAT Advanced Certificate in Bookkeeping – Level 3

AAT Advanced Diploma in Accounting at SCQF – Level 6

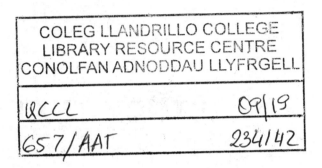
British Library Cataloguing-in-Publication Data

A catalogue record for this book is available from the British Library.

Published by
Kaplan Publishing UK
Unit 2, The Business Centre
Molly Millars Lane
Wokingham
Berkshire
RG41 2QZ

ISBN: 978-1-78740-265-2

CONTENTS

STUDY TEXT

Chapter

KAPLAN PUBLISHING

234142

09118 MI

Kaplan Pul~~lish~~ inding new ways to m~~ake~~ studies and our exciting online resources really do offer something different ~~to students lo~~ ccess.

This book comes with free MyKaplan online resources so that you can study anytime, anywhere. **This free online resource is not sold separately and is included in the price of the book.**

Having purchased this book, you have access to the following online study materials:

CONTENT	AAT	
	Text	Kit
Electronic version of the book	✓	✓
Progress tests with instant answers	✓	
Mock assessments online	✓	✓
Material updates	✓	✓

How to access your online resources

Kaplan Financial students will already have a MyKaplan account and these extra resources will be available to you online. You do not need to register again, as this process was completed when you enrolled. If you are having problems accessing online materials, please ask your course administrator.

If you are not studying with Kaplan and did not purchase your book via a Kaplan website, to unlock your extra online resources please go to www.mykaplan.co.uk/addabook (even if you have set up an account and registered books previously). You will then need to enter the ISBN number (on the title page and back cover) and the unique pass key number contained in the scratch panel below to gain access. You will also be required to enter additional information during this process to set up or confirm your account details.

If you purchased through Kaplan Flexible Learning or via the Kaplan Publishing website you will automatically receive an e-mail invitation to MyKaplan. Please register your details using this email to gain access to your content. If you do not receive the e-mail or book content, please contact Kaplan Publishing.

Your Code and Information

This code can only be used once for the registration of one book online. This registration and your online content will expire when the final sittings for the examinations covered by this book have taken place. Please allow one hour from the time you submit your book details for us to process your request.

Please scratch the film to access your MyKaplan code.

Please be aware that this code is case-sensitive and you will need to include the dashes within the passcode, but not when entering the ISBN. For further technical support, please visit www.MyKaplan.co.uk

INTRODUCTION

HOW TO USE THESE MATERIALS

These Kaplan Publishing learning materials have been carefully designed to make your learning experience as easy as possible and to give you the best chance of success in your AAT assessments.

They contain a number of features to help you in the study process.

The sections on the Unit Guide, the Assessment and Study Skills should be read before you commence your studies.

They are designed to familiarise you with the nature and content of the assessment and to give you tips on how best to approach your studies.

STUDY TEXT

This study text has been specially prepared for the revised AAT qualification introduced in September 2016.

It is written in a practical and interactive style:

- key terms and concepts are clearly defined

- all topics are illustrated with practical examples with clearly worked solutions based on sample tasks provided by the AAT in the new examining style

- frequent activities throughout the chapters ensure that what you have learnt is regularly reinforced

- 'pitfalls' and 'examination tips' help you avoid commonly made mistakes and help you focus on what is required to perform well in your examination

- 'Test your understanding' activities are included within each chapter to apply your learning and develop your understanding

ICONS

The chapters include the following icons throughout.

They are designed to assist you in your studies by identifying key definitions and the points at which you can test yourself on the knowledge gained.

 Definition

These sections explain important areas of knowledge which must be understood and reproduced in an assessment

 Example

The illustrative examples can be used to help develop an understanding of topics before attempting the test your understanding exercises

 Test your understanding

These are exercises which give the opportunity to assess your understanding of all the assessment areas.

Quality and accuracy are of the utmost importance to us so if you spot an error in any of our products, please send an email to mykaplanreporting@kaplan.com with full details.

Our Quality Co-ordinator will work with our technical team to verify the error and take action to ensure it is corrected in future editions.

UNIT GUIDE

Introduction

This Advanced level unit is about preparing final accounts for sole traders and partnerships, and helping students to become aware of alternative business organisation structures.

This purpose of this unit is to provide the background knowledge and skills that a student needs in order to be capable of drafting accounts for sole traders and partnerships, and it provides the background knowledge of the regulations governing company accounts. A successful student will be able to complete tasks while being aware of potential ethical issues and know how to report information effectively. The student should become an accomplished member of the accounting team who is able to work with little supervision and who can see a financial picture of the organisation as a whole.

Students will be able to recognise the different types of organisations that need to prepare financial statements and will understand why such statements are important to users in the business environment. The financial accounting techniques and knowledge that they have already acquired will be developed to prepare accounting records when the records are incomplete, and students will become familiar with mark-up and margin.

Students will recognise special accounting requirements for partnerships. They will become aware of legislation and regulations governing financial statements, and will be able to recall and apply ethical knowledge to situations arising during the preparation of accounts. This unit also introduces students to the terminology and formats used by accountants in the financial statements of companies, working with the International Financial Reporting Standards (IFRS) terminology that is utilised across AAT.

Using all of this, the student will be able to prepare final accounts for sole traders and partnerships from an initial trial balance and present these to their line manager. They will then gain awareness of the more detailed requirements for the preparation of company financial statements.

Final Accounts Preparation is a mandatory unit in this qualification.

It is closely linked to the Advanced level financial accounting unit, Advanced Bookkeeping, as well as to the Foundation level units, Bookkeeping Transactions and Bookkeeping Controls. In addition, it draws on the ethical principles from the Advanced level unit, Ethics for Accountants. On completion of this unit, students are prepared to start the Professional level unit, Financial Statements of Limited Companies.

Learning outcomes

On completion of this unit the learner will be able to:

- Distinguish between the financial recording and reporting requirements of different types of organisation

- Explain the need for final accounts and the accounting and ethical principles underlying their preparation

- Prepare accounting records from incomplete information

- Produce accounts for sole traders

- Produce accounts for partnerships

- Recognise the key differences between preparing accounts for a limited company and a sole trader

Scope of content

Note on the Conceptual Framework

The Conceptual Framework for Financial Reporting 2010 identifies one assumption underlying the preparation of financial statements – the going concern assumption. However, the AAT have confirmed that the unit specification for Final Accounts Preparation departs from this and states that there are two underlying assumptions – going concern and the accruals basis.

To perform this unit effectively you will need to know and understand the following:

Chapter

1   Distinguish between the financial recording and reporting requirements of different types of organisation

1.2	Recognise the regulations applying to different types of organisation	**4**

Students need to know:

- that different regulations apply to different organisations, including awareness of relevant:

  – partnership legislation

  – companies legislation and accounting standards

  – limited liability partnership legislation

  – charity legislation, charity regulators and statements of recommended practice

- that presentation of final accounts for sole traders and partnerships is not governed by statute and accounting regulations to the same extent those for limited companies are; they have no definitive format

- the importance of behaving professionally, being competent and acting with due care at work

- the importance of deadlines in the preparation of final accounts.

		Chapter
2	**Explain the need for final accounts and the accounting and ethical principles underlying their preparation**	
2.1	Describe the primary users of final accounts and their needs	4

- the primary users of final accounts

- the reasons why final accounts are needed by these users.

2.2	Describe the accounting principles underlying the preparation of final accounts	4

- the existence of a framework within which accountants work

- the underlying assumptions governing financial statements: accrual basis, going concern basis

- the fundamental qualitative characteristics of useful financial information

- the supporting qualitative characteristics

- that financial statements should be free from material misstatement.

- recognise circumstances when a business is no longer a going concern and be aware of the effect on the value of its assets

2.3	Apply ethical principles when preparing final accounts	4

Students need to know:

- the importance of behaving professionally and being competent

- the importance of objectivity, including an awareness of the potential for conflicts of interest and bias

- that security and confidentiality of information must be maintained at all times.

Chapter

3   **Prepare accounting records from incomplete information**

3.1   Recognise circumstances where there are incomplete records   **3**

Students need to know:

- possible reasons why information may be missing

- possible reasons for inconsistencies within the records themselves

- examples of the types of figures that may be missing

- the importance of acting with integrity.

3.2   Prepare ledger accounts, using these to estimate missing figures   **3**

Students need to know how to:

- use the content of daybooks, including sales tax

- use information from the cash-book

- distinguish between relevant and non-relevant data

- reconstruct ledger accounts: sales and purchases ledger control accounts, sales tax control account and the bank account, using incomplete information

- calculate and correctly label the missing figure of such reconstructed accounts

- calculate opening or closing balances from information given

- adjust data for sales tax from data provided.

Chapter

3.3	Calculate figures using mark-up and margin	**3**

Students need to know:

- what margin and mark-up are and the difference between them.

Students need to be able to:

- calculate mark-up and margin

- use mark-up and margin to calculate missing figures

- use cost of goods sold to determine a missing figure

- adjust data for sales tax from data provided.

3.4	Assess the reasonableness of given figures within a particular context	**3**

Students need to know how to:

- recognise whether a figure is reasonable in a given context

- explain reasons behind the difference between an actual balance and a calculation

- exercise professional scepticism.

4   Produce accounts for sole traders

4.1	Calculate opening and/or closing capital for a sole trader	**1**

Students need to know be able to:

- account for drawings, capital injections and profits or losses

- record these in ledger accounts

- explain movements in capital balances.

Chapter

4.2 Describe the components of a set of final accounts for a sole trader

1

Students need to know:

- the purpose of a statement of profit or loss

- the purpose of a statement of financial position

- how the statement of financial position is linked to the accounting equation

- how the statement of profit or loss and the statement of financial position are related.

4.3 Prepare a statement of profit or loss for a sole trader in the given format

1

Students need to be able to:

- itemise income and expenditure in line with given organisational policies

- transfer data from the trial balance to the appropriate line of the statement according to the level of detail given for the organisation.

4.4 Prepare a statement of financial position for a sole trader in the given format

1

Students need to be able to:

- apply the net assets presentation of the statement of financial position

- transfer data from the trial balance to the appropriate line of the statement, according to the level of detail given for the organisation.

5 **Produce accounts for partnerships**

5.1 The following points apply to assessment criteria 5.2, 5.4, 5.5, 5.6 and 5.7

- Number of partners is limited to a maximum of three.

- No changes in the partnership during the period.

- Either a profit or loss may be provided for allocation.

Chapter

5.2   Describe the key components of a partnership   **2**
agreement

Students need to know:

- what a partnership agreement typically may or
  may not contain

- that a formal partnership agreement may not
  exist for all partnerships.

5.3   Describe the accounting procedures for a change in   **2**
partners

Students need to know:

- a simple definition of goodwill in accounting
  terms

- why goodwill will change capital balances on
  admission or retirement of a partner

- that goodwill may be introduced and
  subsequently eliminated from the accounting
  records using the profit sharing ratio.

Students need to be able to:

- calculate the goodwill adjustments using the
  profit sharing ratio

- enter such adjustments in ledger accounts and
  balance off these accounts as necessary.

5.4   Describe the key components of partnership   **2**
accounts

Students need to know:

- the purpose of a statement of profit or loss

- the purpose and content of the partnership
  appropriation account

- how the statement of profit or loss is linked to
  the partnership appropriation account

- the nature and content of partners' current
  accounts

- the nature and content of partners' capital
  accounts

- the purpose of a statement of financial position.

Chapter

5.5 Prepare a statement of profit or loss for a partnership, in the given format

2

Students need to know:

- that the statement of profit or loss for a partnership is an adaptation of one for a sole trader.

Students need to know how to:

- itemise income and expenditure in line with given organisational policies

- transfer data from the trial balance to the appropriate line of the statement according to the level of detail given for the organisation.

5.6 Prepare a partnership appropriation account, in compliance with the partnership agreement and in the given format

2

Students need to be able to:

- apply the terms of a partnership agreement

- record interest on capital (but not how to calculate it)

- record interest on drawings (but not how to calculate it)

- record salaries or commission paid to partners

- calculate, and appropriate and account for, the residual profit according to the profit sharing ratio

- recognise that partners' salaries, commission and interest are neither expenses nor income of the partnership

- present this account in the format given for the organisation.

Chapter

5.7   Prepare the current accounts for each partner   **2**

Students need to be able to:

- enter ledger accounting entries

- account for drawings in the form of cash, goods or services

- link the current account with figures from the appropriation account.

5.8   Prepare a statement of financial position for a partnership, in compliance with the partnership agreement and in the given format   **2**

Students need to know:

- that the statement of financial position for a partnership is an adaptation of one for a sole trader.

Students need to be able to:

- apply the net assets presentation of the statement of financial position

- transfer data from the trial balance to the appropriate line of the statement according to the level of detail given for the organisation

- show partners' current and capital accounts on the statement of financial position.

Chapter

6   **Recognise the key differences between preparing accounts for a limited company and a sole trader**

6.1   Describe the main sources of regulation governing company accounts   **4**

Students need to know:

- the particular importance of maintaining an up-to-date knowledge of relevant legislation and accounting standards that apply to companies

- which source provides the required formats for the statement of profit or loss and statement of financial performance for a company adopting IFRS

- which standards provide guidance for property, plant and equipment, and inventories, where IFRS is adopted (recalled as examples of regulation).

6.2   Describe the more detailed reporting arising from these regulations   **4**

Students need to know:

- the requirement to prepare financial statements at least annually and file them publicly

- that selection and application of accounting policies is regulated, and the objectives that should be met when developing them

- that limited company financial statements need to follow statutory formats, with prescribed headings and terminology

- that cost of sales and other expenses must be classified according to rules

- that taxation is charged in the statement of profit or loss of a company

- that only the carrying value of non-current assets appears on the statement of financial position of a company

- that notes must be provided as part of the financial statements of a company.

Delivering this unit

Unit Name	Content links	Suggested order of delivery
Advanced Bookkeeping	This unit builds on the knowledge and skills acquired from studying Advanced Bookkeeping.	It is recommended that Final Accounts Preparation is delivered after Advanced Bookkeeping.
Ethics for Accountants	Ethics and ethical principles are embedded within this unit.	It is recommended that Final Accounts Preparation is delivered either at the same time as or after Ethics for Accountants.
Management Accounting: Costing. Spreadsheets for Accounting and Indirect Tax	Three Advanced level units – Management Accounting: Costing, Spreadsheets for Accounting and Indirect Tax – have links to Final Accounts Preparation.	Not applicable.

KAPLAN PUBLISHING

THE ASSESSMENT

Test specification for this unit

Assessment type	Marking type	Duration of exam
Computer based unit assessment	Computer marked	2 hours

The assessment for this unit consists of 6 compulsory tasks.

The competency level for AAT assessments is 70%.

Learning outcomes		Weighting
1	Distinguish between the financial recording and reporting requirements of different types of organisation	10%
2	Explain the need for final accounts and the accounting and ethical principles underlying their preparation	7%
3	Prepare accounting records from incomplete information	27%
4	Produce accounts for sole traders	31%
5	Produce accounts for partnerships	20%
6	Recognise the key differences between preparing accounts for a limited company and a sole trader	5%
Total		**100%**

UNIT LINK TO THE SYNOPTIC ASSESSMENT

AAT AQ16 introduced a Synoptic Assessment, which students must complete if they are to achieve the appropriate qualification upon completion of a qualification. In the case of the Advanced Diploma in Accounting, students must pass all of the mandatory assessments and the Synoptic Assessment to achieve the qualification.

As a Synoptic Assessment is attempted following completion of individual units, it draws upon knowledge and understanding from those units. It may be appropriate for students to retain their study materials for individual units until they have successfully completed the Synoptic Assessment for that qualification.

With specific reference to this unit, the following learning objectives are also relevant to the Advanced Diploma in Accounting Synoptic Assessment:

LO1   Distinguish between the financial recording and reporting requirements of different types of organisation

LO2   Explain the need for final accounts and the accounting and ethical principles underlying their preparation

LO3   Prepare accounting records from incomplete information

LO4   Produce accounts for sole traders

LO5   Produce accounts for partnerships

LO6   Recognise the key differences between preparing accounts for a limited company and a sole trader

STUDY SKILLS

Preparing to study

Devise a study plan

Determine which times of the week you will study.

Split these times into sessions of at least one hour for study of new material. Any shorter periods could be used for revision or practice.

Put the times you plan to study onto a study plan for the weeks from now until the assessment and set yourself targets for each period of study – in your sessions make sure you cover the whole course, activities and the associated questions in the workbook at the back of the manual.

If you are studying more than one unit at a time, try to vary your subjects as this can help to keep you interested and see subjects as part of wider knowledge.

When working through your course, compare your progress with your plan and, if necessary, re-plan your work (perhaps including extra sessions) or, if you are ahead, do some extra revision/practice questions.

Effective studying

Active reading

You are not expected to learn the text by rote, rather, you must understand what you are reading and be able to use it to pass the assessment and develop good practice.

A good technique is to use SQ3Rs – Survey, Question, Read, Recall, Review:

1 Survey the chapter

Look at the headings and read the introduction, knowledge, skills and content, so as to get an overview of what the chapter deals with.

2 Question

Whilst undertaking the survey ask yourself the questions you hope the chapter will answer for you.

3   Read

Read through the chapter thoroughly working through the activities and, at the end, making sure that you can meet the learning objectives highlighted on the first page.

4   Recall

At the end of each section and at the end of the chapter, try to recall the main ideas of the section/chapter without referring to the text. This is best done after a short break of a couple of minutes after the reading stage.

5   Review

Check that your recall notes are correct.

You may also find it helpful to re-read the chapter to try and see the topic(s) it deals with as a whole.

Note taking

Taking notes is a useful way of learning, but do not simply copy out the text.

The notes must:

- be in your own words
- be concise
- cover the key points
- be well organised
- be modified as you study further chapters in this text or in related ones.

Trying to summarise a chapter without referring to the text can be a useful way of determining which areas you know and which you don't.

Three ways of taking notes

1   Summarise the key points of a chapter

2   Make linear notes

A list of headings, subdivided with sub-headings listing the key points.

If you use linear notes, you can use different colours to highlight key points and keep topic areas together.

Use plenty of space to make your notes easy to use.

KAPLAN PUBLISHING

3   Try a diagrammatic form

The most common of which is a mind map.

To make a mind map, put the main heading in the centre of the paper and put a circle around it.

Draw lines radiating from this to the main sub-headings which again have circles around them.

Continue the process from the sub-headings to sub-sub-headings.

Annotating the text

You may find it useful to underline or highlight key points in your study text – but do be selective.

You may also wish to make notes in the margins.

Revision phase

Kaplan has produced material specifically designed for your final examination preparation for this unit.

These include pocket revision notes and a bank of revision questions specifically in the style of the new syllabus.

Further guidance on how to approach the final stage of your studies is given in these materials.

Further reading

In addition to this text, you should also read the 'Accounting Technician' magazine every month to keep abreast of any guidance from the examiners.

KAPLAN PUBLISHING

Preparation of accounts for a sole trader

1

Introduction

For Final Accounts Preparation you need to be able to prepare the financial statements; a statement of profit or loss and a statement of financial position for a sole trader.

These financial statements may be prepared directly from the extended trial balance or from a trial balance plus various adjustments.

In this chapter we will consider the step by step approach to the financial statements preparation, firstly from an extended trial balance and then directly from an initial trial balance.

The knowledge for this unit has been acquired in Advanced Bookkeeping but within this unit, you will be expected to apply the skills to complete the financial statements.

ASSESSMENT CRITERIA	CONTENTS
Calculate opening and/or closing capital for a sole trader (4.1)	1 Statement of profit or loss for a sole trader
Describe the components of a set of final accounts for a sole trader (4.2)	2 The statement of financial position for a sole trader
Prepare a statement of profit or loss for a sole trader in the given format (4.3)	3 Preparing financial statements from the trial balance
Prepare a statement of financial position for a sole trader in the given format (4.4)	

1 Statement of profit or loss for a sole trader

1.1 Introduction

In Advanced Bookkeeping we considered in outline the layout of a statement of profit or loss for a sole trader. Now we will consider it in more detail.

1.2 Statement of profit or loss

Technically the statement of profit or loss is split into two elements:

- the trading account to determine gross profit;
- the statement of profit or loss to determine net profit.

However, in general the whole statement is referred to as the statement of profit or loss. The statement of profit or loss shows business performance over a specific period of time, the accounting period.

1.3 Trading account

The trading account calculates the gross profit or loss that has been made from the trading activities of the sole trader – the buying and selling of goods.

 Definition

The gross profit (or loss) is the profit (or loss) from the trading activities of the sole trader.

The trading account looks like this:

	£	£
Revenue		X
Less: Cost of goods sold		
Opening inventory	X	
Purchases	X	
	──	
	X	
Less: Closing inventory	(X)	
	──	(X)
		──
Gross profit (loss)		X
		──

1.4 Profit or loss

The remaining content of the statement of profit or loss is a list of the expenses of the business. These are deducted from the gross profit to give the profit for the year (or the net profit).

Q Definition

The net profit or loss is the profit or loss after deduction of all of the expenses of the business.

Test your understanding 1

Statement of profit or loss for the year ended 31 December 20X2.

Calculate the revenue and cost of goods sold (complete the boxes).

	£	£
Revenue		[ ]
Less: Cost of goods sold		
Opening inventory	37,500	
Purchases	158,700	
	196,200	[ ]
Less: Closing inventory	(15,000)	
Gross profit		111,300

A typical statement of profit or loss is shown below.

Statement of profit or loss of Stanley for the year-ended 31 December 20X2

	£	£
Revenue		X
Less: Cost of goods sold		
Inventory on 1 January (opening inventory)	X	
Add: Purchases of goods	X	
	X	
Less: Inventory on 31 December (closing inventory)	(X)	
		(X)
Gross profit		X
Sundry income:		
Discounts received	X	
Commission received	X	
Rent received	X	
Interest received	X	
		X
		X
Less: Expenses:		
Rent	X	
Rates	X	
Lighting and heating	X	
Telephone	X	
Postage	X	
Insurance	X	
Stationery	X	
Payroll expenses	X	
Depreciation	X	
Accountancy and audit fees	X	
Bank charges and interest	X	
Irrecoverable debts	X	
Allowance for doubtful debts adjustment	X	
Delivery costs	X	
Van running expenses	X	
Selling expenses	X	
Discounts allowed	X	
		(X)
Profit/(loss) for the year		X/(X)

1.5 Preparation of the statement of profit or loss

The statement of profit or loss is prepared by listing all of the entries from the ETB that are in the profit or loss columns.

 Example

Given below is the final ETB for Lyttleton

Account name	Trial balance Dr £	Trial balance Cr £	Adjustments Dr £	Adjustments Cr £	Profit or loss statement Dr £	Profit or loss statement Cr £	Statement of fin. pos. Dr £	Statement of fin. pos. Cr £
Capital		7,830						7,830
Cash	2,010						2,010	
Non-current assets	9,420						9,420	
Accumulated depreciation		3,470		942				4,412
SLCA	1,830						1,830	
Open. inventory	1,680				1,680			
PLCA		390						390
Sales		14,420				14,420		
Purchases	8,180			1,500	6,680			
Rent	1,100		100		1,200			
Electricity	940		400		1,340			
Rates	950			200	750			
Depreciation expense			942		942			
Allowance for doubtful debts adjustments			55		55			
Allowance for doubtful debts				55				55
Drawings			1,500				1,500	
Accruals				500				500
Prepayments			200				200	
Closing inventory SoFP			1,140				1,140	
Closing inventory I/S				1,140		1,140		
Profit					2,913			2,913
	26,110	**26,110**	**4,337**	**4,337**	**15,560**	**15,560**	**16,100**	**16,100**

We will now show how the final statement of profit or loss for Lyttleton would look.

Solution

Statement of profit or loss of Lyttleton for the year-ended 31 December 20X5

		£	£
Revenue			14,420
Less:	Cost of goods sold		
	Opening inventory	1,680	
	Purchases	6,680	
		8,360	
Less:	Closing inventory	(1,140)	
			(7,220)
Gross profit			7,200
Less: Expenses			
	Rent	1,200	
	Electricity	1,340	
	Rates	750	
	Depreciation	942	
	Allowance for doubtful debts increase	55	
Total expenses			(4,287)
Net profit for the year			2,913

All of the figures in the statement of profit or loss columns in the ETB have been used to prepare this statement of profit or loss.

The final net profit is the profit figure calculated as a balancing figure in the ETB.

2 The statement of financial position for a sole trader

2.1 Introduction

We have considered the statement of financial position in outline in the Accounts Preparation unit and now we will consider it in more detail.

> **Definition**
>
> A statement of financial position is a list of the assets and liabilities of the sole trader at the end of the accounting period.

The assets are split into non-current assets and current assets.

> **Definition**
>
> Non-current assets are assets that will be used within the business over a long period (usually greater than one year), e.g. land and buildings

> **Definition**
>
> Current assets are assets that are expected to be realised within the business in the normal course of trading (usually a period less than one year) e.g. inventory.

The liabilities are split into current liabilities and non-current liabilities.

> **Definition**
>
> Current liabilities are the short term payables of a business. This generally means payables that are due to be paid within twelve months of the statement of financial position date e.g. trade payables

> **Definition**
>
> Non-current liabilities are payables that will be paid over a longer period, which is normally in excess of one year, e.g. loans

An example of a typical sole trader's statement of financial position is given below:

Statement of financial position of Stanley at 31 December 20X2

	Cost £	Depreciation £	£
Non-current assets			
Freehold factory	X	X	X
Machinery	X	X	X
Motor vehicles	X	X	X
	X	X	X
Current assets			
Inventory		X	
Trade receivables	X		
Less: Allowance for doubtful debts	(X)		
		X	
Prepayments		X	
Cash at bank		X	
Cash in hand		X	
		X	
Current liabilities			
Trade payables	X		
Accruals	X		
		(X)	
Net current assets			X
Total assets less current liabilities			X
Non-current liabilities			
12% loan			(X)
Net assets			X
Capital at 1 January			X
Net profit for the year			X
			X
Less: Drawings			(X)
Proprietor's funds			X

2.2 Assets and liabilities

The assets and liabilities in a formal statement of financial position are listed in a particular order:

- firstly the non-current assets less the accumulated depreciation (remember that this net total is known as the carrying amount). It should be noted that when preparing final accounts for a limited company, only the carrying amounts of the non-current assets are shown on the face of the statement of financial position. A breakdown of the cost and accumulated depreciation for each type of asset are shown in the notes to the accounts.

- next the current assets in the following order – inventory, receivables, prepayments then bank and cash balances

- next the current liabilities – payables and accruals that are payable within 12 months

- finally the long-term payables such as loan accounts.

The assets are all added together and the liabilities are then deducted. This gives the statement of financial position total.

2.3 Capital balances

The total of the assets less liabilities of the sole trader should be equal to the capital of the sole trader.

The capital is shown in the statement of financial position as follows:

	£
Opening capital at the start of the year	X
Add: Net profit/(loss) for the year	X
	X
Less: Drawings	(X)
Closing capital	X

This closing capital should equal the total of all of the assets less all liabilities, as shown in the accounting equation assets – liabilities = capital. (NB: this formula can be rearranged as assets = capital + liabilities).

The capital balance represents the owner's funds, i.e. what the owner will be left with if the business is wound up and all the assets are sold and all the liabilities paid off.

Example

Given below is the completed ETB for Lyttleton. This time the statement of financial position will be prepared.

Account name	Trial balance Dr £	Trial balance Cr £	Adjustments Dr £	Adjustments Cr £	Income statement Dr £	Income statement Cr £	Statement of fin. pos. Dr £	Statement of fin. pos. Cr £
Capital		7,830						7,830
Cash	2,010						2,010	
Non-current assets	9,420						9,420	
Accumulated depreciation		3,470		942				4,412
SLCA	1,830						1,830	
Inventory	1,680			1,680				
PLCA		390						390
Revenue		14,420				14,420		
Purchases	8,180			1,500	6,680			
Rent	1,100		100		1,200			
Electricity	940		400		1,340			
Rates	950			200	750			
Depreciation expense			942		942			
Allowance for doubtful debts adjustments			55		55			
Allowance for doubtful debts				55				55
Drawings			1,500				1,500	
Accruals				500				500
Prepayments			200				200	
Closing inventory: P&L				1,140		1,140		
Closing inventory: SoFP			1,140				1,140	
Profit (15,560 – 12,647)					2,913			2,913
	26,110	26,110	4,337	4,337	15,560	15,560	16,100	16,100

Each of the assets and liabilities that appear in the statement of financial position columns will appear in the statement of financial position.

Solution

Statement of financial position of Lyttleton at 31 December 20X5

	Cost £	Accumulated dep'n £	£
Non-current assets	9,420	4,412	5,008
Current assets			
Inventory		1,140	
Trade receivables	1,830		
Less: Allowance for doubtful debts	(55)		
		1,775	
Prepayments		200	
Cash		2,010	
		5,125	
Less:			
Current liabilities			
Payables	390		
Accruals	500		
		(890)	
Net current assets			4,235
Net assets			9,243
Capital 1 January			7,830
Net profit for the year			2,913
			10,743
Less: Drawings			(1,500)
Proprietor's funds			9,243

Note

- the non-current assets are shown at their carrying amounts;

- the current assets are sub-totalled as are the current liabilities – the current liabilities are then deducted from the current assets to give net current assets;

- the net current assets are added to the non-current asset carrying amount to reach the statement of financial position total, net assets.

The statement of financial position total of net assets should be equal to the closing capital; the statement of financial position is then said to balance (it used to be referred to as a 'balance sheet'). If your statement of financial position does not balance then make some quick checks, such as basic arithmetic and missing figures. Do not spend too much time searching for your error as the time can be better used on the rest of the examination. If you have time left over at the end then you can return to the question to look for the error.

 Test your understanding 2

Given below is a completed extended trial balance.

Extended trial balance at 31 December 20X6

Account name	Trial balance Dr £	Trial balance Cr £	Adjustments Dr £	Adjustments Cr £	Statement of profit or loss Dr £	Statement of profit or loss Cr £	Statement of fin. pos. Dr £	Statement of fin. pos. Cr £
Fittings	7,300						7,300	
Accumulated depreciation 1.1.X6		2,500		400				2,900
Leasehold	30,000						30,000	
Accumulated depreciation 1.1.X6		6,000		1,000				7,000
Inventory 1 January 20X6	15,000				15,000			
Sales ledger control account	10,000			500			9,500	
Allowance for doubtful debts 1.1.X6		800	515					285
Cash in hand	50						50	
Cash at bank	1,250						1,250	
Purchases ledger control account		18,000						18,000
Capital		19,050						19,050
Drawings	4,750		1,200				5,950	
Purchases	80,000			1,200	78,800			
Revenue		120,000				120,000		
Wages	12,000			200	11,800			
Advertising	4,000		200		4,200			
Rates	1,800			360	1,440			
Bank charges	200				200			
Depreciation charge			1,400		1,400			

Allowance for doubtful debts adjustments				515		515	
Irrecoverable debts			500		500		
Prepayments			360				360
Closing inventory SoFP			21,000				21,000
Closing inventory P&L				21,000		21,000	
					113,340	141,515	
Net profit					28,175		28,175
	166,350	166,350	25,175	25,175	141,515	141,515	75,410	75,410

Prepare the statement of profit or loss for the business.

Pick the appropriate account heading from the options below.

Statement of profit or loss for the year-ended 31 December 20X6

	£	£

Revenue

Less: Cost of goods sold

    Opening inventory/Closing inventory/Purchases

    Purchases/Opening inventory/Closing inventory

                         ————

    Opening inventory/Closing inventory/Purchases

                         ————

Gross profit

Less: Expenses

    Trade receivables/Wages

    Advertising/Prepayments

    Drawings/Rates

    Bank charges/Capital

    Depreciation charge

    Allowance for doubtful debts adjustment

    Irrecoverable debts

Total expenses

Profit for the year

Prepare the statement of financial position for the business.

Pick the appropriate account heading from the options below.

Statement of financial position as at 31 December 20X6

	£	£	£

Non-current assets:
Fittings/Closing inventory
Trade receivables/Leasehold

_____ _____ _____

_____ _____

Current assets:
Closing inventory/Opening inventory
Trade payables/Trade receivables
Less: Allowance for doubtful debts

_____

Accruals/Prepayments
Cash at bank/Drawings
Capital/Cash in hand

_____

Current liabilities:
Trade receivables/Trade payables

_____

_____

_____

Owner's capital
Capital at 1.1.X6
Drawings/Net profit for the year
Less: Capital/Drawings

_____

_____

3 Preparing financial statements from the trial balance

3.1 Introduction

As we have seen in Accounts Preparation, the extended trial balance is a useful working paper for the eventual preparation of the financial statements of a sole trader. However, in the examination you may well be required to prepare a set of financial statements directly from the trial balance.

In this section we will work through a comprehensive example which will include the extraction of the initial trial balance, correction of errors and clearing a suspense account, accounting for year-end adjustments and finally the preparation of the financial statements.

Example

Given below are the balances taken from a sole trader's ledger accounts on 31 March 20X4

	£
Sales ledger control account	30,700
Telephone	1,440
Purchases ledger control account	25,680
Heat and light	2,480
Motor vehicles at cost	53,900
Computer equipment at cost	4,500
Carriage inwards	1,840
Carriage outwards	3,280
Wages	67,440
Loan interest	300
Capital	48,000
Drawings	26,000
Allowance for doubtful debts	450
Bank overdraft	2,880
Purchases	126,800
Petty cash	50
Revenue	256,400
Insurance	3,360
Accumulated depreciation – motor vehicles	15,000
Accumulated depreciation – computer equipment	2,640
Inventory at 1 April 20X3	13,200
Loan	8,000
Rent	23,760

The following information is also available:

(i)   The value of inventory at 31 March 20X4 was £14,400.

(ii)   Motor vehicles are to be depreciated at 30% on reducing balance basis and computer equipment at 20% on cost.

(iii) A telephone bill for £180 for the three months to 31 March 20X4 did not arrive until after the trial balance had been drawn up.

(iv)   Of the insurance payments, £640 is for the year-ending 31 March 20X5.

(v)   An irrecoverable debt of £700 is to be written off and an allowance of 2% is required against the remaining receivables.

Solution

Step 1

The first stage is to draw up the initial trial balance. Remember that assets and expenses are debit balances and liabilities and income are credit balances.

	£	£
Sales ledger control account	30,700	
Telephone	1,440	
Purchases ledger control account		25,680
Heat and light	2,480	
Motor vehicles at cost	53,900	
Computer equipment at cost	4,500	
Carriage inwards	1,840	
Carriage outwards	3,280	
Wages	67,440	
Loan interest	300	
Capital		48,000
Drawings	26,000	
Allowance for doubtful debts		450
Bank overdraft		2,880
Purchases	126,800	
Petty cash	50	
Revenue		256,400
Insurance	3,360	
Accumulated depreciation – motor vehicles		15,000
Accumulated depreciation – computer equipment		2,640
Inventory at 1 April 20X3	13,200	
Loan		8,000
Rent	23,760	
	359,050	359,050

Step 2

Now to deal with the year-end adjustments:

(a) The value of inventory at 31 March 20X4 was £14,400.

Closing inventory – profit or loss			
	£		£
		Closing inventory statement of financial position	14,400

Closing inventory – statement of financial position			
	£		£
Closing inventory income statement	14,400		

- We now have the closing inventory for the statement of profit or loss.

(b) The motor vehicles and computer equipment have yet to be depreciated for the year. Motor vehicles are depreciated at 30% on reducing balance basis and computer equipment at 20% on cost.

Motor vehicles depreciation (53,900 − 15,000) × 30% = £11,670

Computer equipment depreciation 4,500 × 20% = £900

Depreciation charge			
	£		£
Accumulated depreciation – motor vehicles	11,670	Balance c/d	12,570
Accumulated depreciation – computer equipment	900		
	12,570		12,570
Balance b/d	12,570		

Accumulated depreciation account – motor vehicles			
	£		£
		Balance b/d	15,000
Balance c/d	26,670	Depreciation expense	11,670
	26,670		26,670
		Balance b/d	26,670

Accumulated depreciation account – computer equipment

	£		£
		Balance b/d	2,640
Balance c/d	3,540	Depreciation expense	900
	———		———
	3,540		3,540
	———		———
		Balance b/d	3,540

(c) A telephone bill for £180 for the three months to 31 March 20X4 did not arrive until after the trial balance had been drawn up.

This needs to be accrued for:

Debit	Telephone	£180
Credit	Accruals	£180

Telephone account

	£		£
Balance b/d	1,440		
Accrual	180	Balance c/d	1,620
	———		———
	1,620		1,620
	———		———
Balance b/d	1,620		

Accruals

	£		£
		Telephone	180

(d) Of the insurance payments £640 is for the year-ending 31 March 20X5.

This must be adjusted for as a prepayment:

Debit	Prepayment	£640
Credit	Insurance account	£640

Prepayments

	£		£
Insurance	640		

Insurance account

	£		£
Balance b/d	3,360	Prepayment	640
		Balance c/d	2,720
	3,360		3,360
Balance b/d	2,720		

(e) An irrecoverable debt of £700 is to be written off and an allowance of 2% is required against the remaining receivables.

Firstly, the irrecoverable debt must be written off in order to find the amended balance on the sales ledger control account.

Debit   Irrecoverable debts expense   £700

Credit   Sales ledger control account   £700

Irrecoverable debts expense account

	£		£
Sales ledger control account	700		

Sales ledger control account

	£		£
Balance b/d	30,700	Irrecoverable debts expense	700
		Balance c/d	30,000
	30,700		30,700
Balance b/d	30,000		

Now we can determine the allowance for doubtful debts required at £30,000 × 2% = £600. The balance on the allowance account in the trial balance is £450, therefore an increase of £150 is required.

Debit   Allowance for doubtful debts adjustment (P&L)   £150

Credit   Allowance for doubtful debts account (SoFP)   £150

Allowance for doubtful debts adjustment account

	£		£
Allowance for doubtful debts	150	Balance c/d	150
	———		———
	150		150
	———		———
Balance b/d	150		

Allowance for doubtful debts account

	£		£
		Balance b/d	450
Balance c/d	600	Allowance for doubtful debts adjustment	150
	———		———
	600		600
	———		———
		Balance b/d	600

Step 5

Now that all of the adjustments have been put through the ledger accounts, an amended trial balance can be drawn up as a check and as a starting point for preparing the financial statements.

Remember to consider the adjustments just identified when preparing the trial balance.

Trial balance at 31 March 20X4

	£	£
Sales ledger control account	30,000	
Telephone	1,620	
Purchases ledger control account		25,680
Heat and light	2,480	
Motor vehicles at cost	53,900	
Computer equipment at cost	4,500	
Carriage inwards	1,840	
Carriage outwards	3,280	
Wages	67,440	
Loan interest	300	
Capital		48,000
Drawings	26,000	
Allowance for doubtful debts		600
Bank overdraft		2,880
Purchases	126,800	
Petty cash	50	
Revenue		256,400
Insurance	2,720	
Accumulated depreciation – motor vehicles		26,670
Accumulated depreciation – computer equipment		3,540
Inventory at 1 April 20X3	13,200	
Loan		8,000
Rent	23,760	
Inventory at 31 March 20X4	14,400	14,400
Depreciation charge	12,570	
Accruals		180
Prepayments	640	
Allowance for doubtful debt adjustment	150	
Irrecoverable debts expense	700	
	386,350	386,350

Step 6

We are now in a position to prepare the financial statements for the sole trader. Take care with the carriage inwards and carriage outwards. They are both expenses of the business but carriage inwards is treated as part of cost of goods sold, whereas carriage outwards is one of the list of expenses.

Statement of profit or loss for the year-ended 31 March 20X4

	£	£
Revenue		256,400
Less: Cost of goods sold		
Opening inventory	13,200	
Carriage inwards	1,840	
Purchases	126,800	
	———	
	141,840	
Less: Closing inventory	(14,400)	
	———	127,440
		———
Gross profit		128,960
Less: Expenses		
Telephone	1,620	
Heat and light	2,480	
Carriage outwards	3,280	
Wages	67,440	
Loan interest	300	
Insurance	2,720	
Rent	23,760	
Depreciation charge	12,570	
Irrecoverable debts	700	
Allowance for doubtful debts adjustment	150	
	———	
Total expenses		115,020
		———
Profit for the year		13,940
		———

KAPLAN PUBLISHING

Statement of financial position as at 31 March 20X4

	Cost	Accumulated depreciation	Carrying amount
	£	£	£
Non-current assets			
Motor vehicles	53,900	26,670	27,230
Computer equipment	4,500	3,540	960
	58,400	30,210	28,190
Current assets			
Inventory		14,400	
Trade receivables	30,000		
Less: Allowance for doubtful debts	(600)		
		29,400	
Prepayment		640	
Petty cash		50	
		44,490	
Current liabilities			
Bank overdraft	2,880		
Trade Payables	25,680		
Accruals	180		
		28,740	
Net current assets			15,750
Total assets less current liabilities			43,940
Non-current liability:			
Loan			(8,000)
Net assets			35,940
Capital			
Opening capital			48,000
Net profit for the year			13,940
			61,940
Less: Drawings			26,000
Proprietor's funds			35,940

Test your understanding 3

Given below is the list of ledger balances for a sole trader at 30 June 20X4 after all year-end adjustments have been put through.

	£
Revenue	165,400
Sales ledger control account	41,350
Wages	10,950
Bank	1,200
Rent	8,200
Capital	35,830
Purchases ledger control account	15,100
Purchases	88,900
Electricity	1,940
Telephone	980
Drawings	40,000
Inventory at 1 July 20X3	9,800
Motor vehicles at cost	14,800
Accumulated depreciation – motor vehicles	7,800
Fixtures at cost	3,200
Accumulated depreciation – fittings	1,800
Accruals	100
Prepayments	210
Inventory at 30 June 20X4 – statement of financial position	8,300
Inventory at 30 June 20X4 – statement of profit or loss	8,300
Depreciation charge	4,500

You are required to:

(i) Draw up a trial balance to check that it balances (you should find that the trial balance does balance).

(ii) Prepare the financial statements for the sole trader for the year-ending 30 June 20X4.

(i) **Trial balance as at 30 June 20X4**

	£	£
Revenue		
Sales ledger control account		
Wages		
Bank		
Rent		
Capital		
Purchases ledger control account		
Purchases		
Electricity		
Telephone		
Drawings		
Inventory at 1 July 20X3		
Motor vehicles at cost		
Accumulated depreciation – motor vehicles		
Fixtures at cost		
Accumulated depreciation fittings		
Accruals		
Prepayments		
Inventory at 30 June 20X4 – SFP		
Inventory at 30 June 20X4 – SPL		
Depreciation charge		

(ii) **Statement of profit or loss for the year-ending 30 June 20X4**

	£	£
Revenue		
Less: Cost of goods sold		
	_____	
Less:	_____	
		_____
Gross profit		
Less: Expenses		
	_____	
Total expenses		
		_____
Net profit		
		_____

Statement of financial position as at 30 June 20X4

	Cost £	Depreciation £	CV £
Non-current assets			
	———	———	———
	———	———	———
Current assets			
		———	
Current liabilities			
	———		
		———	
Net current assets			
			———
Net assets			
			———
Capital			
Net profit for the year			
			———
Drawings			
			———
Proprietor's funds			
			———

Test your understanding 4

Tick as appropriate.

1   Opening inventory is recorded in the statement of profit or loss as

     An expense   ☐

     Cost of goods sold   ☐

2   Indicate where the drawings should be shown in the financial statements

     Profit or loss expenses   ☐

     Statement of financial position as a deduction to capital   ☐

3   Payroll expenses are recorded as

     A liability in the statement of financial position   ☐

     An expense in the statement of profit or loss   ☐

4   Does the allowance for doubtful debt adjustment appear in the statement of profit or loss or the statement of financial position?

     Statement of profit or loss   ☐

     Statement of financial position   ☐

5   Irrecoverable debt expenses are recorded in the statement of financial position as an increase in the allowance for doubtful debts

     True   ☐

     False   ☐

Test your understanding 5

David Pedley

The following information is available for David Pedley's business for the year-ended 31 December 20X8. He started his business on 1 January 20X8.

	£
Payables	6,400
Receivables	5,060
Purchases	16,100
Revenue	28,400
Motor van	1,700
Drawings	5,100
Insurance	174
General expenses	1,596
Rent and rates	2,130
Salaries	4,162
Inventory at 31 December 20X8	2,050
Sales returns	200
Cash at bank	2,628
Cash in hand	50
Capital introduced	4,100

Required:

Prepare a statement of profit or loss for the year-ended 31 December 20X8 and a statement of financial position at that date.

Test your understanding 6

Karen Finch

On 1 April 20X7 Karen Finch started a business with capital of £10,000 which she paid into a business bank account.

The following is a summary of the cash transactions for the first year.

	£
Amounts received from customers	17,314
Salary of assistant	2,000
Cash paid to suppliers for purchases	10,350
Purchase of motor van on 31 March 20X8	4,000
Drawings during the year	2,400
Amounts paid for electricity	560
Rent and rates for one year	1,100
Postage and stationery	350

At the end of the year, Karen was owed £4,256 by her customers and owed £5,672 to her suppliers. She has promised her assistant a bonus for the year of £400. At 31 March 20X8 this had not been paid.

At 31 March 20X8 there was closing inventory of £4,257 and the business owed £170 for electricity for the last quarter of the year. A year's depreciation is to be charged on the motor van at 25% on cost.

Required:

Prepare a statement of profit or loss for the year-ended 31 March 20X8 and a statement of financial position at that date.

Test your understanding 7

The trial balance of Elmdale at 31 December 20X8 is as follows

	Dr £	Cr £
Capital		8,602
Inventory	2,700	
Revenue		21,417
Purchases	9,856	
Rates	1,490	
Drawings	4,206	
Electricity	379	
Freehold shop	7,605	
Receivables	2,742	
Payables		3,617
Cash at bank		1,212
Cash in hand	66	
Sundry expenses	2,100	
Wages and salaries	3,704	
	34,848	34,848

In addition, Elmdale provides the following information:

(i) Closing inventory has been valued for accounts purposes at £3,060.

(ii) An electricity bill amounting to £132 in respect of the quarter to 28 February 20X9 was paid on 7 March 20X9.

(iii) Rates include a payment of £1,260 made on 10 April 20X8 in respect of the year to 31 March 20X9.

Tasks

(a) Show the adjustments to the ledger accounts for the end-of-period adjustments (i) to (iii).

(b) Prepare a statement of profit or loss for the year-ended 31 December 20X8.

4 Summary

The unit Prepare Final Accounts for Sole Traders and Partnerships requires the preparation of the financial statements for a sole trader.

The statement of profit or loss for the period summarises the transactions in the period and leads to a net profit or loss for the period.

The statement of financial position lists the assets and liabilities of the business on the last day of the accounting period in a particular order.

If you have to prepare the financial statements from an extended trial balance then each balance will already have been classified as either a profit or loss item or a statement of financial position item.

If you are preparing the financial statements from a trial balance, you will have to recognise whether the balances should appear in the statement of profit or loss or in the statement of financial position.

Test your understanding answers

Test your understanding 1

Statement of profit or loss extract for the year-ended 31 December 20X2

Calculate the sales and cost of goods sold.

	£	£
Revenue		292,500
Less: Cost of goods sold		
Opening inventory	37,500	
Purchases	158,700	
	196,200	
Less: Closing inventory	(15,000)	
		(181,200)
Gross profit		111,300

Test your understanding 2

Statement of profit or loss for the year-ended 31 December 20X6

	£	£
Revenue		120,000
Less: Cost of goods sold		
Opening inventory	15,000	
Purchases	78,800	
	93,800	
Less: Closing inventory	(21,000)	
		(72,800)
Gross profit		47,200

Less: Expenses

	£
Wages	11,800
Advertising	4,200
Rates	1,440
Bank charges	200
Depreciation charge	1,400
Allowance for doubtful debts adjustment	(515)
Irrecoverable debts	500

Total expenses	**(19,025)**
Profit for the year	**28,175**

Statement of financial position at 31 December 20X6

	£	£	£
Non-current assets			
Fittings	7,300	2,900	4,400
Leasehold	30,000	7,000	23,000
	37,300	9,900	27,400
Current assets			
Inventory		21,000	
Trade receivables	9,500		
Less: Allowance for doubtful debts	(285)		
		9,215	
Prepayments		360	
Cash at bank		1,250	
Cash in hand		50	
		31,875	
Current liabilities			
Trade payables		(18,000)	
Net current assets			13,875
Net assets			41,275
Owner's capital			
Capital at 1.1.X6			19,050
Net profit for the year			28,175
Less: Drawings			(5,950)
Proprietor's funds			41,275

Test your understanding 3

(i)   Trial balance as at 30 June 20X4

	£	£
Revenue		165,400
Sales ledger control account	41,350	
Wages	10,950	
Bank	1,200	
Rent	8,200	
Capital		35,830
Purchases ledger control account		15,100
Purchases	88,900	
Electricity	1,940	
Telephone	980	
Drawings	40,000	
Inventory at 1 July 20X3	9,800	
Motor vehicles at cost	14,800	
Accumulated depreciation – motor vehicles		7,800
Fixtures at cost	3,200	
Accumulated depreciation – fittings		1,800
Accruals		100
Prepayments	210	
Inventory at 30 June 20X4 – SPL		8,300
Inventory at 30 June 20X4 – SFP	8,300	
Depreciation charge	4,500	
	234,330	234,330

(ii) **Statement of profit or loss for the year-ending 30 June 20X4**

	£	£
Revenue		165,400
Less: Cost of goods sold		
Opening inventory	9,800	
Purchases	88,900	
	98,700	
Less: Closing inventory	(8,300)	
		(90,400)
Gross profit		75,000
Less: Expenses		
Wages	10,950	
Rent	8,200	
Electricity	1,940	
Telephone	980	
Depreciation charge	4,500	
Total expenses		(26,570)
Net profit		48,430

Statement of financial position as at 30 June 20X4

	Cost £	Depreciation £	CV £
Non-current assets			
Motor vehicles	14,800	7,800	7,000
Fittings	3,200	1,800	1,400
	18,000	9,600	8,400
Current assets			
Inventory		8,300	
Trade receivables		41,350	
Prepayments		210	
Bank		1,200	
		51,060	
Current liabilities			
Trade payables	15,100		
Accruals	100		
		(15,200)	
Net current assets			35,860
Net assets			44,260
Capital			35,830
Net profit for the year			48,430
			84,260
Drawings			(40,000)
Proprietor's funds			44,260

Test your understanding 4

1   Opening inventory is recorded in the statement of profit or loss as

Cost of goods sold

2   Indicate where the drawings should be shown in the financial statements

Statement of financial position

3   Payroll expenses are recorded as

An expense in the statement of profit or loss

4   Does the allowance for doubtful debt adjustment appear in the statement of profit or loss or statement of financial position?

Statement of profit or loss

5   Irrecoverable debt expenses are recorded in the statement of financial position as an increase in the allowance for doubtful debts

False

Test your understanding 5

David Pedley

Statement of profit or loss for the year ended 31 December 20X8

	£	£
Sales		28,400
Less: Returns		(200)
		28,200
Opening inventory	–	
Purchases	16,100	
Less: Closing inventory	(2,050)	
Cost of goods sold		(14,050)
Gross profit		14,150
Salaries	4,162	
Rent and rates	2,130	
Insurance	174	
General expenses	1,596	
Total expenses		(8,062)
Profit for the year		6,088

Statement of financial position as at 31 December 20X8

	£	£
Non-current assets		
Motor van		1,700
Current assets		
Closing inventory	2,050	
Trade receivables	5,060	
Cash at bank	2,628	
Cash in hand	50	
	9,788	
Trade payables	(6,400)	
Net current assets		3,388
Net assets		5,088

Capital account

Capital introduced	4,100
Profit for the year (per income statement)	6,088
Less: Drawings	(5,100)
	———
Proprietor's funds	5,088
	———

📝 Test your understanding 6

Karen Finch

Statement of profit or loss for the year ended 31 March 20X8

	£	£
Revenue (£17,314 + £4,256)		21,570
Purchases (£10,350 + £5,672)	16,022	
Closing inventory	(4,257)	
	———	(11,765)
Gross profit		9,805
Assistant's salary plus bonus (£2,000 + £400)	2,400	
Electricity (£560 + £170)	730	
Rent and rates	1,100	
Postage and stationery	350	
Depreciation charge	1,000	
	———	
Total expenses		(5,580)
		———
Profit for the year		4,225
		———

Statement of financial position at 31 March 20X8

	£	£
Non-current assets		
Motor van at cost		4,000
Accumulated depreciation		(1,000)
		―――――
Carrying amount		3,000
Current assets		
Inventory	4,257	
Trade receivables	4,256	
Cash (W1)	6,554	
	―――――	
	15,067	
	―――――	
Current liabilities		
Trade payables	5,672	
Accruals (400 + 170)	570	
	―――――	
	6,242	
	―――――	
Net current assets		8,825
		―――――
Net assets		11,825
		―――――
Capital		10,000
Capital introduced at 1 April 20X7		
Profit for the year	4,225	
Less Drawings	(2,400)	
	―――――	
Retained profit for the year		1,825
		―――――
Proprietors funds		11,825
		―――――

Test your understanding 7

(a) Ledger accounts

(i)   Closing inventory (I/S)

	£		£
Balance to income statement	3,060	Closing inventory SoFP	3,060

Closing inventory (SoFP)

	£		£
Closing inventory P&L	3,060	Balance c/d	3,060
	3,060		3,060
Balance b/d	3,060		

(ii)   Electricity

	£		£
Per trial balance	379	Profit or loss	423
Accrual	44		
	423		423

Rates

	£		£
Per trial balance	1,490	Profit or loss	1,175
		Prepayment	315
	1,490		1,490

Points to note:

- As regards electricity the accrual of £44 is shown on the statement of financial position as a current liability and increases the charge to profit or loss for electricity for expenses incurred but not yet paid.

- The rates prepayment of £315 is shown on the statement of financial position as a current asset and reduces the charge to profit or loss. This reflects the fact that some of the expense recorded relates to the next accounting year.

KAPLAN PUBLISHING

(b)

Elmdale

Statement of profit or loss for the year ended

31 December 20X8

	£	£
Revenue		21,417
Opening inventory	2,700	
Purchases	9,856	
	12,556	
Closing inventory	(3,060)	
Cost of goods sold		9,496
Gross profit		11,921
Rates	1,175	
Electricity	423	
Wages and salaries	3,704	
Sundry expenses	2,100	
Total expenses		7,402
Profit for the year		4,519

Partnership accounts

2

Introduction

For Final Accounts Preparation you need to apply acquired knowledge and skills from Advanced Bookkeeping to prepare a set of partnership accounts.

You need to be able to prepare a statement of profit or loss for a partnership, which is no different to that for a sole trader, then prepare a partnership appropriation account and a statement of financial position for the partnership.

You also need to be able to deal with events such as the admission of a new partner or the retirement of a partner.

All of this will be dealt with in this chapter.

ASSESSMENT CRITERIA	CONTENTS
Describe the key components of a partnership agreement, including partnership appropriation account, goodwill, partners' capital and current accounts, and statement of financial position (5.1), (5.3)	1 Accounting for partner's capital and profits
	2 Appropriation of profit
Describe the accounting procedures for a change in partners (5.2)	3 Changes in the partnership agreement
Prepare a statement of profit or loss for a partnership, in the given format (5.4)	4 Admission of a new partner
	5 Retirement of a partner
Prepare a partnership appropriation account, in compliance with the partnership agreement and in the given format (5.5)	6 Preparing financial statements for a partnership
Prepare the current accounts for each partner (5.6)	
Prepare a statement of financial position for a partnership, in compliance with the partnership agreement and in the given format (5.7)	

1 Accounting for partner's capital and profits

1.1 What is a partnership?

> ### 🔍 Definition
>
> A partnership is where two or more people carry on business together with a view to making a profit and sharing that profit.

In a partnership each of the partners will introduce capital into the business and each partner will have a share in the profits of the business.

1.2 Partnership capital

Each of the partners in a partnership will invest capital into the business in just the same way that a sole trader does.

In a partnership accounting system it is important to keep the capital paid in by each partner separate so that there is a record of how much the business owes back to each of the partners.

In order to keep a record of the capital invested by each partner a separate capital account for each partner is kept in the general ledger.

> ### 🔍 Definition
>
> A capital account in a partnership is an account for each partner which records the capital that they have invested into the business.

When a partner invests capital into the business the double entry is:

Dr   Bank account

Cr   Partner's capital account

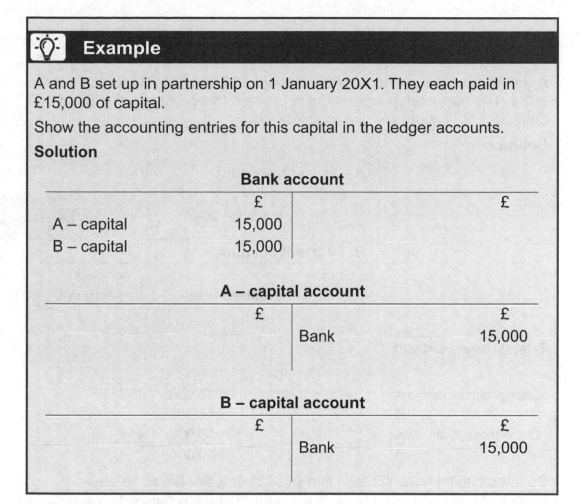

Example

A and B set up in partnership on 1 January 20X1. They each paid in £15,000 of capital.

Show the accounting entries for this capital in the ledger accounts.

Solution

Bank account

	£		£
A – capital	15,000		
B – capital	15,000		

A – capital account

	£		£
		Bank	15,000

B – capital account

	£		£
		Bank	15,000

1.3 Partnership profits

When a partnership makes a profit or a loss for an accounting period then this must be shared between the partners.

Usually there will be a partnership agreement which sets out what percentage of the profit each partner is to receive.

If there is no written partnership agreement then the Partnership Act 1890 states that profits should be shared equally between all of the partners.

1.4 Accounting for partnership profits

The profit that each partner is due from the business is recorded in individual current accounts.

Definition

The partners' current accounts record the amount of profit that is due to each partner from the business. This is not to be confused with the bank account of the same name.

Example

A and B, from the previous example, earn £20,000 of profit for the year 20X1. The partnership agreement is to share this profit equally. Show their current accounts for the year 20X1.

Solution

A – current account

	£			£
			Profit for year	10,000

B – current account

	£			£
			Profit for year	10,000

Trial balance extract

		Dr	Cr
Capital accounts	– A		15,000
	– B		15,000
Current accounts	– A		10,000
	– B		10,000

Both the capital accounts and current accounts are credit balances as these are amounts owed back to the partners by the business, i.e. special payables of the business.

The credit balance in the partners' current accounts is the same as the credit balance for 'net profit for the year' on the bottom half of the sole trader statement of financial position. It represents the funds due to the proprietors.

1.5 Drawings

Just as a sole trader takes money and/or goods out of the business, then partners will do exactly the same thing. If a partner withdraws cash the double entry would be:

Dr Partner's current account

Cr Bank account

If they withdraw inventory the double entry would be:

Dr Partner's current account

Cr Purchases

Example

In the year 20X1 partner A had drawings of £6,000 and partner B drawings of £8,000. Show how these transactions would appear in the current accounts of the partners and what balances would be shown in the trial balance.

Solution

A – current account

	£		£
Drawings	6,000	Profit for year	10,000
Balance c/d	4,000		
	–––––		–––––
	10,000		10,000
	–––––		–––––
		Balance b/d	4,000

B – current account

	£		£
Drawings	8,000	Profit for year	10,000
Balance c/d	2,000		
	–––––		–––––
	10,000		10,000
	–––––		–––––
		Balance b/d	2,000

Trial balance extract

		Dr	Cr
Capital accounts	– A		15,000
	– B		15,000
Current accounts	– A		4,000
	– B		2,000

1.6 Columnar accounts

In some partnerships the ledger accounts for capital and current accounts are produced in columnar form which means that each partner has a column in a joint capital and current account.

Example

Using the previous example of A and B we will see how their capital and current accounts would look if the ledger accounts were in columnar form.

Solution

Capital accounts

	A £	B £		A £	B £
			Bank	15,000	15,000

Current accounts

	A £	B £		A £	B £
Drawings	6,000	8,000	Profit for year	10,000	10,000
Balance c/d	4,000	2,000			
	10,000	10,000		10,000	10,000
			Balance b/d	4,000	2,000

Remember that the capital account is only used for recording the capital paid into the business by each partner. The profit earned and the drawings made by each partner are recorded in the current accounts.

 Test your understanding 1

Continuing with the partnership of A and B, in the year 20X2 A paid a further £5,000 of capital into the business.

The profit of the business for the year was £28,000 and this is to be shared equally between A and B.

During the year A had cash drawings of £12,000 and B had cash drawings of £13,000.

Record these transactions in the capital and current accounts of A and B and show the balances on these accounts that would appear in the trial balance at the end of 20X2.

Capital account – A

	£		£
		Balance b/d	15,000
	___		___
	___		___

Capital account – B

	£		£
		Balance b/d	15,000
	___		___
	___		___

Current account – A

	£		£
		Balance b/d	4,000
	___		___
	___		___

Current account – B

	£		£
		Balance b/d	2,000
	___		___
	___		___

Trial balance extract

	Dr £	Cr £
Capital account – A		
Capital account – B		
Current account – A		
Current account – B		

1.7 Debit balances on current accounts

In some instances a partner may withdraw more in cash drawings than is owing to him out of accumulated profits. In this case the partner's current account will show a debit balance.

 Example

Suppose that the balance on a partner's current account at the start of the year is a credit balance of £3,000.

His share of profit for the year is £17,000 and he has £22,000 of drawings.

Show the partner's current account for the year.

Solution

Current account

	£		£
Drawings	22,000	Balance b/d	3,000
		Profit share	17,000
		Balance c/d	2,000
	_____		_____
	22,000		22,000
	_____		_____
Balance b/d	2,000		

The balance on the current account is a debit balance and would be shown in the trial balance as such.

Always assume that any balances given for partners' current accounts are credit balances unless you are specifically told otherwise.

2 Appropriation of profit

2.1 Appropriation account

We have already seen how the profit of a partnership business is split between the partners in the business according to their profit sharing ratio and is credited to their current accounts.

The actual splitting up of the profit is done in a profit appropriation account. This can either take the form of another ledger account or it can be shown vertically.

2.2 Salaries

In some partnership agreements it is specified that one or more partners will receive a salary to reflect their level of work in the partnership. This is part of the appropriation of profit and must take place before the profit share.

2.3 Sales commission

In some partnership agreements it is specified that the partners will receive commission on their sales made during the year. This is part of the appropriation of profit and must take place before the profit share.

2.4 Interest on capital

As partners will often have contributed different amounts of capital into the partnership, again the partnership agreement may specify that a rate of interest is allowed to each partner on their outstanding balances. This is part of the appropriation of the profit for the period and must take place before the final profit share. **AAT have confirmed that the calculation of interest on capital will not be required in the assessment but the amounts will still need to be recorded.**

2.5 Drawings

Drawings do not go through the appropriation account, they are instead debited to the current accounts but during the year they will be recorded in a drawings account for each partner and then transferred to the current account at the year end. This represents a reduction in the partner's capital.

2.6   Interest on drawings

To penalise those partners who take out drawings from the business, the partnership may charge interest on drawings. Interest may be charged on all drawings or only those above a certain level. This results in a reduction in the amount of profit that the partner is allocated. **AAT have confirmed that the calculation of interest on drawings will not be required in the assessment but the amounts will still need to be recorded.**

A proforma appropriation account is shown below for a partnership with two partners A and B for the year-ended 31 Dec 20X7. Note this is to illustrate the layout of the account and the figures have been included purely for the purposes of the illustration.

	Year ended 31 Dec 20X7 £	Total £
Net profit		100,000
Salaries		
A	–	
B	(12,000)	(12,000)
Sales commission		
A	(1,000)	
B	(2,000)	(3,000)
Interest on capital		
A	(5,000)	
B	(7,000)	(12,000)
Interest on drawings		
A	5,000	
B	–	5,000
Profit available for distribution		78,000
Profit share		
A	(39,000)	
B	(39,000)	(78,000)
Balance		Nil

Note

1   There are five categories of appropriations that can be entered into the appropriation account

    (a)   Salaries

    (b)   Sales commission

    (c)   Interest on capital

    (d)   Interest on drawings

    (e)   Profit share

2   If any of the categories change during the year then it is easier to have two columns for the periods when the change takes place which are then combined in the total column. The column headings might look as follows.

	1 Jan 20X7 to 30 Sept 20X7	1 Oct 20X7 to 31 Dec 20X7	Total

We shall study an example of this later in the chapter.

Example

X, Y and Z are in partnership sharing profits in the ratio 3:2:1

The profits for the year to 30 June 20X7 were £100,000.

Z receives a salary of £12,000 per annum.

The partners' capital accounts have balance b/d of £50,000, £30,000 and £10,000 respectively. Interest for the year is calculated as 5% of the capital balance b/d.

Produce the appropriation account for the year.

Solution

	Year ended 30 June 20X7 £	Total £
Net profit		100,000
Salaries:		
X		
Y		
Z	(12,000)	(12,000)
Interest on capital		
X (50,000 × 5%)	(2,500)	
Y (30,000 × 5%)	(1,500)	
Z (10,000 × 5%)	(500)	(4,500)
Profit available for distribution		83,500
Profit share		
X (83,500 × 3/6)	(41,750)	
Y (83,500 × 2/6)	(27,833)	
Z (83,500 × 1/6)	(13,917)	(83,500)
Balance		Nil

Example

A and B are in partnership sharing profits equally and, for the year 20X1, the partnership made a profit of £20,000.

We will show how the partnership profit is appropriated in both a ledger appropriation account and a vertical appropriation account.

Solution

Ledger appropriation account

The net profit of the partnership is shown as a credit balance, amount owing to the partners, in the appropriation account.

Appropriation account

	£		£
		Balance b/d	20,000

A journal entry will then be put through for the split of the profit.

Debit Appropriation account – A's profit	£10,000
Debit Appropriation account – B's profit	£10,000
Credit A's current account	£10,000
Credit B's current account	£10,000

The appropriation account and the current accounts can then be written up:

Appropriation account

	£		£
Current account – A	10,000	Balance b/d	20,000
Current account – B	10,000		
	———		———
	20,000		20,000
	———		———

Current accounts

	A £	B £		A £	B £
			Appropriation account	£10,000	£10,000

Vertical appropriation account

	£
Net profit for the year	20,000
	———
Profit share – A	10,000
Profit share – B	10,000
	———
	20,000
	———

Example

C and D are in partnership and their capital balances are £100,000 and £60,000 respectively.

During 20X4 the profit made by the partnership totalled £80,000.

The partnership agreement specifies the following:

- D receives a salary of £15,000 per annum.

- Both partners receive interest on their capital balances at the rate of 5%.

- The profit sharing ratio is 2:1.

We will now appropriate the profit and write up the partners' current accounts.

C made £37,000 of drawings during the year and D made £33,500 of drawings during the year.

The balance b/ds on their current accounts were both £1,000 credit balances.

Solution

The salary and the interest on capital must be deducted first from the available profits.

The remainder is then split in the profit share ratio of 2:1.

This means that C gets two thirds of the remaining profit whilst D gets one third of the remaining profit.

Appropriation account

		£	£
Profit for the year			80,000
Salary	– D	15,000	
Interest on capital	– C (100,000 × 5%)	5,000	
	D (60,000 × 5%)	3,000	
		———	(23,000)
			———
Profit available for profit share			57,000
			———
Profit share	– C (57,000 × 2/3)		38,000
	D (57,000 × 1/3)		19,000
			———
			57,000
			———

The current accounts can now be written up to reflect the profit share and the drawings for the year.

Current account

	C £	D £		C £	D £
Drawings	37,000	33,500	Balance b/d	1,000	1,000
			Salary		15,000
			Interest on capital	5,000	3,000
Balance c/d	7,000	4,500	Profit share	38,000	19,000
	44,000	38,000		44,000	38,000
			Balance b/d	7,000	4,500

 Example

Hamish and Campbell started a business on 1 January 20X6, investing £20,000 and £14,000 respectively.

In the first year of trade, the business made £25,000 profit.

They have set up the following partnership agreement:

- Neither partner receives a salary.

- Interest on capital is to be provided at 4%.

- Interest on drawings is to be charged at 2%.

- The balance of profit is to be split in the ratio 3:2.

Both Hamish and Campbell withdrew £5,000 from the business on 1 July 20X6.

Show how this information appears in the partners' capital and current accounts and in the statement of financial position.

Solution

	Year ended 31 Dec X6 £	Total £
Net profit		25,000
Interest on capital		
Hamish	(800)	
Campbell	(560)	(1,360)
Interest on drawings (W)		
Hamish	50	
Campbell	50	100
Profit available for distribution		23,740
Profit share		
Hamish	(14,244)	
Campbell	(9,496)	(23,740)
Balance		Nil

Working – interest on drawings £5,000 × 2% × 6/12 = 50

Hamish total: £800 − £50 + £14,244 = £14,994

Campbell total: £560 - £50 + £9,496 = £10,006

Capital account

	Hamish £	Campbell £		Hamish £	Campbell £
Bal c/d	20,000	14,000	01.01.X6	20,000	14,000
	20,000	14,000		20,000	14,000
			Bal b/d	20,000	14,000

Current account

	Hamish £	Campbell £		Hamish £	Campbell £
Drawings	5,000	5,000	Profit share	14,994	10,006
Bal c/d	9,994	5,006			
	14,994	10,006		14,994	10,006
			Bal b/d	9,994	5,006

Statement of financial position extract:

			£	£
Capital accounts:	Hamish		20,000	
	Campbell		14,000	
				34,000
Current accounts:	Hamish		9,994	
	Campbell		5,006	
				15,000
				49,000

✎ Test your understanding 2

Nick and Ted are in partnership sharing profits in the ratio of 3:2. During the year ended 30 June 20X4 the partnership made a profit of £120,000.

The partnership agreement states that Ted is to receive a salary of £20,000 and that interest on capital balances is paid at 6% per annum. Both Nick and Ted are entitled to 2.5% commission on their sales for the year, provided that their sales exceed £45,000.

The balances on the current accounts, capital accounts and drawings accounts at the year-end before the appropriation of profit were as follows:

		£
Capital	– Nick	150,000
	Ted	100,000
Current	– Nick	3,000 (credit)
	Ted	1,000 (debit)
Drawings	– Nick	56,000
	Ted	59,000
Sales	– Nick	82,400
	Ted	48,600

Complete the appropriation account and the partners' current accounts after appropriation of profit and transfer of drawings at 30 June 20X4.

Appropriation account

		£	£
Net profit			
Salary	– Ted		
Sales commission	– Nick		
	Ted		
Interest on capital	– Nick		
	Ted		
		_____	
			_____
Profit available			
			_____
Profit share	– Nick		
	Ted		
			_____
			_____

Current accounts

	Nick £	Ted £		Nick £	Ted £
Balance b/d			Balance b/d		
Drawings			Salary		
			Sales commission		
			Interest on capital		
Balance c/d			Profit share		
	_____	_____		_____	_____
	_____	_____		_____	_____
			Balance b/d		

2.7 Partnership losses

Any salaries and interest on capital must be appropriated first to the partners even if the partnership makes a loss or if this appropriation turns a profit into a loss.

Then the loss itself is split between the partners in the profit share ratio by debiting their current accounts. The partners suffer the loss in the same proportion they share the profits.

Example

The partnership of E and F made a profit of £10,000 for the year ended 31 March 20X5.

The partnership agreement states that each partner receives interest on their capital balances of 10% per annum and that E receives a salary of £8,000.

Any remaining profits or losses are split in the ratio of 3:1.

The balances on their capital accounts were £50,000 and £40,000 respectively and neither partner had a balance b/d on their current accounts.

Neither partner made any drawings during the year.

Write up the partnership profit appropriation account and the partners' current accounts for the year.

Appropriation account

			£	£
Partnership profit				10,000
Salary	–	E	8,000	
Interest	–	E	5,000	
		F	4,000	
			———	
				(17,000)
				———
Loss to be shared				(7,000)
				———
Loss share	–	E (7,000 × 3/4)		(5,250)
		F (7,000 × 1/4)		(1,750)
				———
				(7,000)
				———

Current account

	E £	F £		E £	F £
Loss share	5,250	1,750	Salary	8,000	
Balance c/d	7,750	2,250	Interest	5,000	4,000
	———	———		———	———
	13,000	4,000		13,000	4,000
	———	———		———	———
			Balance b/d	7,750	2,250

Example

A and B each have current account balances of £10,000.

During 20X1 A had drawings of £6,000 and B had drawings of £8,000.

Show how these are entered in the ledger accounts.

Solution

At the year end the drawings accumulated in the drawings accounts are transferred by a journal entry to the current accounts of the partners as follows:

Debit Current account – A	£6,000
Debit Current account – B	£8,000

Credit Drawings account – A	£6,000
Credit Drawings account – B	£8,000

Drawings account – A

	£		£
Cash	6,000	Current account	6,000

Drawings account – B

	£		£
Cash	8,000	Current account	8,000

Current accounts

	A £	B £		A £	B £
Drawings	6,000	8,000	Balance b/d	10,000	10,000

3 Changes in the partnership agreement

3.1 Changes in profit share

In some partnerships the partners will decide to change the partnership agreement and the profit share ratio part of the way through the year. In these cases the appropriation of profit must take place in two separate calculations.

Firstly, the profit for the period under the old profit share agreement must be appropriated using the old profit share ratio.

Secondly, the profit for the period after the change must be appropriated using the new profit share ratio.

Unless otherwise stated, it must be assumed that profits accrue evenly throughout the year (i.e. divide the total profit/loss for the year by 12 to work out a monthly profit/loss).

 Example

Bill and Ben are in partnership and the profits of the partnership for the year ended 31 December 20X3 were £60,000.

The partnership agreement at the start of the year was that profits were to be shared equally.

However, on 31 March 20X3 it was decided to change the partnership agreement so that Ben received a salary of £8,000 per annum and the remaining profits were shared in the ratio of 2:1.

Both partners had a balance b/d on their current accounts of £2,000 (credit) and the profits for the year accrued evenly.

Show the appropriation of the profits to the partners' current accounts for the year.

Solution

Step 1

Determine the profit for the first three months of the year and appropriate that according to the old profit share ratio.

	£
Profit (£60,000 × 3/12)	15,000
Bill (15,000 × 1/2)	7,500
Ben (15,000 × 1/2)	7,500
	15,000

Step 2

Determine the profit for the final nine months of the year and appropriate that according to the new profit share ratio.

Profit (£60,000 × 9/12)	45,000
Salary – Ben (£8,000 × 9/12)	(6,000)
Profit to be appropriated	39,000
Profit share – Bill (£39,000 × 2/3)	26,000
Ben (£39,000 × 1/3)	13,000
	39,000

Example

Consider the previous example and write up the appropriation account for the same information in a columnar form

Solution

	1 Jan – 31 Mar 20X3	1 Apr – 31 Dec 20X3	Total (£)
Profit	**15,000**	**45,000**	**60,000**
Salary			
Ben (£8,000 × 9/12)		6,000	6,000
Profit available for distribution	**15,000**	**39,000**	**54,000**
Profit share			
Bill	7,500	26,000	33,500
Ben	7,500	13,000	20,500
Balance	**Nil**	**Nil**	**Nil**

3.2 Changes in interest

The partnership agreement may be changed during a period so that for example a different rate of interest is paid on capital from a given date in the year.

The profit must be divided into the two periods and interest must be calculated both before and after that date.

Example

A, B and C are in partnership for the year ended 31 December 20X8, sharing profits in the ratio 3:2:1. The net profit for the year was £90,000.

At 1 January 20X8 the partners' capital was

	£
A	50,000
B	30,000
C	20,000

For the period to 30 April 20X8, the partners received interest at 3% on their capital at the beginning of the year. For the remainder of the year they received interest at 4% on their capital at the beginning of the year. Profits accrued evenly throughout the year.

Task 1

Complete the table showing the interest received by the partners during the year for the two separate periods and in total

	1 Jan X8 – 30 Apr X8 £	1 May X8 – 31 Dec X8 £	Total £

Task 2

Prepare the appropriation account for the year to 31 December 20X8.

Solution

Task 1

	1 Jan X8 – 30 Apr X8 £	1 May X8 – 31 Dec X8 £	Total £
Interest			
A	50,000 × 3% × 4/12 = 500	50,000 × 4% × 8/12 = 1,333	1,833
B	30,000 × 3% × 4/12 = 300	30,000 × 4% × 8/12 = 800	1,100
C	20,000 × 3% × 4/12 = 200	20,000 × 4% × 8/12 = 533	733

Task 2

Appropriation account for the year to 31 December 20X8

	1 Jan X8 – 30 Apr X8 £	1 May X8 – 31 Dec X8 £	Total £
Net profit	**30,000**	**60,000**	**90,000**
A	500	1,333	1,833
B	300	800	1,100
C	200	533	733
Profit available for distribution	**29,000**	**57,334**	**86,334**
Profit share			
A	29,000 × 3/6 = 14,500	57,334 × 3/6 = 28,667	43,167
B	29,000 × 2/6 = 9,667	57,334 × 2/6 = 19,111	28,778
C	29,000 × 1/6 = 4,833	57,334 × 1/6 = 9,556	14,389
Balance	**Nil**	**Nil**	**Nil**

Test your understanding 3

During the year ended 30 June 20X4, the partnership of Jill, Jane and Jan made a profit of £100,000.

Up until 31 March 20X4 the profit share ratio was 2:2:1

However, the partnership agreement was changed on 31 March 20X4 so that Jane was to receive a salary of £16,000 per annum and that the profits were to be shared equally.

The balances on the partners' current accounts and drawings accounts at 30 June 20X4 were as follows:

			£
Current accounts	–	Jill	3,000
		Jane	2,000
		Jan	1,000
Drawings accounts	–	Jill	38,000
		Jane	40,000
		Jan	25,000

Prepare the appropriation account and the partners' current accounts for the year. Assume that profits accrued evenly throughout the year.

Appropriation account

	£
Profit to 31 March 20X4	_____
Profit share – Jill	
Jane	
Jan	_____
	_____
Profit to 30 June 20X4	
Salary Jane	_____
Profit available	
	_____
Profit share – Jill	
Jane	
Jan	_____
	_____

Current accounts

	Jill	Jane	Jan		Jill	Jane	Jan
	£	£	£		£	£	£
Drawings				Balance b/d			
				Profit share			
				Salary			
Balance c/d				Profit share			
				Balance c/d			
	___	___	___		___	___	___
	___	___	___		___	___	___
Balance b/d				Balance b/d			

3.3 Changes in salary, interest and profit share

The partnership agreement may be changed during a period so that all three variables (salary, interest and profit share) are altered during the period.

The profit must be divided into the two periods (assuming that all the changes are effective from the same day in the period) and any changes put into the appropriate period.

Example

X, Y and Z are in partnership for the year ended 31 December 20X8.

At the start of the year they share profits in the ratio 2:2:1. The net profit for the year was £144,000.

At 1 January 20X8 the partners' capital was

	£
X	100,000
Y	50,000
Z	40,000

For the period to 31 May 20X8, the partners received interest at 3% on their capital at the beginning of the year.

For the remainder of the year they received interest at 4% on their capital at the beginning of the year.

For the period to 31 May 20X8 Z received a salary of £18,000 per annum. For the remainder of the year Z received no salary and the profit share was changed to 3:2:2.

During the year the partners each drew £2,000 per month in drawings.

Task 1

Complete the table showing the interest received by the partners during the year for the two separate periods and in total.

	1 Jan 0X – 31 May X8 £	1 June X8 – 31 Dec X8 £	Total £

Task 2

Complete the table showing the appropriation account for the partnership for both periods down to the line for the 'profits available for distribution'.

	1 Jan X8 – 31 May X8 £	1 June X8 – 31 Dec X8 £	Total £
Net profit			
Salaries			
X			
Y			
Z			
Interest			
X			
Y			
Z			
Profits available for distribution			

Task 3

Complete the appropriation account showing the profit shares for the partners and the balance left for distribution if any.

Task 4

Explain how drawings are entered in the books of accounts.

Solution

Task 1

	1 Jan X8 – 31 May X8 £	1 June X8 – 31 Dec X8 £	Total £
Interest			
X	100,000 × 3% × 5/12 = 1,250	100,000 × 4% × 7/12 = 2,333	3,583
Y	50,000 × 3% × 5/12 = 625	50,000 × 4% × 7/12 = 1,167	1,792
Z	40,000 × 3% × 5/12 = 500	40,000 × 4% × 7/12 = 933	1,433

Task 2 and 3

Appropriation account for the year to 31 December 2008

	1 Jan X8 – 31 May X8 £	1 June X8 – 31 Dec X8 £	Total £
Net profit	**60,000**	**84,000**	**144,000**
Salaries			
X			
Y			
Z (18,000 × 5/12)	7,500		7,500
Interest			
X	1,250	2,333	3,583
Y	625	1,167	1,792
Z	500	933	1,433
Profit available for distribution	**50,125**	**79,567**	**129,692**
Profit share			
X	(50,125 × 2/5) 20,050	(79,567 × 3/7) 34,100	54,150
Y	(50,125 × 2/5) 20,050	(79,567 × 2/7) 22,733	42,783
Z	(50,125 × 1/5) 10,025	(79,567 × 2/7) 22,734	32,759
Balance	**Nil**	**Nil**	**Nil**

Task 4

Drawings are not an expense of the business or a form of remuneration for the partners.

They are simply the partners taking money out of the business on account of the profit share that they will eventually receive.

The drawings are therefore not entered in the partnership statement of profit or loss, but are entered as a debit in the partners' current accounts.

4 Admission of a new partner

4.1 Introduction

When a new partner is admitted to the partnership then the partners will agree a certain sum of cash that the new partner must pay for his share in the partnership. The basic double entry for the cash that the new partner brings into the partnership is:

Debit   Bank account

Credit   New partner's capital account

However, there is a complication in that we need to consider the goodwill of the partnership.

4.2 Goodwill

As well as the net assets that a partnership have recorded in their ledger accounts such as machinery, motor vehicles, receivables, inventory, payables, etc., most businesses will have another asset which is not recorded in the ledger accounts, being goodwill.

Goodwill comes about due to the excellence or reputation of the business. It can be due to good quality products, good after sales service, good location, excellence of employees and many other factors.

The problem with goodwill is that not only is it very difficult to measure in monetary terms but it is also very volatile.

Goodwill is essentially the value of the business as a whole over and above the value of the recorded net assets. Unless the business is actually being sold then this total value is only an estimate.

A further problem is the nature of goodwill. Suppose that the goodwill of a restaurant business has been built up due to the reputation of the head chef; if that chef leaves or there is a bout of food poisoning in the restaurant, the goodwill is wiped out immediately.

Due to these problems, such goodwill is not recognised in the financial statements of a business. However, there is little doubt that it does exist in many businesses.

4.3 Goodwill and admission of a new partner

When a new partner is admitted to a partnership he will be buying not only a share of the recorded net assets of the business but also a share of the unrecorded goodwill in the business.

This must be recognised in the accounting procedures.

Step 1

Immediately before the admission of the new partner, the amount of goodwill that the old partners have built up must be recognised and shared out between the partners. This is done by the following double entry:

Debit   Goodwill account with the estimated value of the goodwill

Credit Old partners' capital accounts in the old profit share ratio

Step 2

The new partner will now be admitted and the cash that he brings into the partnership is accounted for by:

Debit   Bank account

Credit New partner's capital account

Step 3

Finally the goodwill must be eliminated from the books. This is done by:

Debit   New partners' capital accounts in the new profit share ratio

Credit Goodwill account with the value of the goodwill

By this stage the goodwill has been taken out of the accounts again and the partners' capital account balances have been adjusted to account for the old partners' share of the goodwill they have earned and the new partner's purchase of not only a share of the recorded net assets but also his share of the unrecorded asset goodwill.

 Example

Pete and Paul have been in partnership for a number of years sharing profits equally.

The balance on Pete's capital account is £100,000 and the balance on Paul's capital account is £80,000.

They have decided to admit a new partner to the partnership, Phil. Phil will contribute £60,000 in cash to the partnership on his admission and the profit share ratio after he is admitted will be two fifths of profits for Pete and Paul and one fifth of profits for Phil.

The goodwill in the partnership is estimated to be £30,000.

Write up the partners' capital accounts to reflect the admission of Phil.

Solution

Step 1

Set up the (temporary) goodwill account and credit the old partners in the old profit share ratio in their capital accounts.

Goodwill account

	£		£
Capital accounts	30,000		

Capital accounts

	Pete	Paul		Pete	Paul
	£	£		£	£
			Balance b/d	100,000	80,000
			Goodwill	15,000	15,000

Step 2

Introduce the new partner and his capital

Capital accounts

	Pete £	Paul £	Phil £		Pete £	Paul £	Phil £
				Bal b/d	100,000	80,000	
				Goodwill	15,000	15,000	
				Bank			60,000

(NB: the bank T account is not shown).

Step 3

Eliminate the goodwill by debiting all of the partners' capital accounts in the new profit share ratio and crediting the goodwill account.

Goodwill account

	£		£
Capital accounts	30,000	Capital accounts	30,000

Capital accounts

	Pete £	Paul £	Phil £		Pete £	Paul £	Phil £
Goodwill	12,000	12,000	6,000	Bal b/d	100,000	80,000	
				Goodwill	15,000	15,000	
Bal c/d	103,000	83,000	54,000	Bank			60,000
	115,000	95,000	60,000		115,000	95,000	60,000
				Bal b/d	103,000	83,000	54,000

What has happened here is that with his £60,000 Phil has purchased a share of the recorded net assets of the business worth £54,000 and £6,000 of goodwill, as shown by his capital account.

He has effectively purchased this from Pete and Paul for £3,000 each as their capital balances have increased by £3,000 in total each.

Test your understanding 4

Karl and Len have been in partnership for a number of years sharing profits in the ratio of 2:1.

They have capital account balances of £80,000 and £50,000 respectively.

On 30 June 20X4 they have invited Nina to join the partnership and she is to introduce £35,000 of capital.

From this date the profits are to be shared with two fifths to Karl and Len and one fifth to Nina. The goodwill of the partnership at 30 June 20X4 is estimated to be £15,000.

Write up the partners' capital accounts to reflect the admission of Nina.

Capital accounts

	Karl £	Len £	Nina £		Karl £	Len £	Nina £
	___	___	___		___	___	___
	___	___	___		___	___	___

5 Retirement of a partner

5.1 Introduction

When a partner retires from a partnership the full amounts that are due to him must be calculated. This will include his capital account balance, his current account balance plus his share of any goodwill that the partnership has at the retirement date. The adjustments in the partners' capital accounts to reflect all of this are very similar to those for the admission of a new partner.

5.2 Accounting adjustments

On the retirement of a partner there are a number of accounting adjustments that must take place to ensure that the full amounts due to the retiring partner are paid to him.

Step 1

Transfer the retiring partner's current account balance to his capital account so that we are only dealing with one account.

Debit   Partners' current account balance

Credit Partners' capital account

Step 2

Recognise the goodwill that has been built up in the partnership by temporarily setting up a goodwill account and crediting all of the partners with their share of the goodwill.

Debit   Goodwill account with the value of the goodwill on the retirement date

Credit Partners' capital accounts in their profit sharing ratio

Step 3

Now the retiring partner has the total balance that is due to him in his capital account. He must then be paid off. The simplest method is to pay him what is due to him in cash:

Debit   Retiring partner's capital account with the balance due

Credit Bank account

The partnership may not have enough cash to pay off all that is due to the partner so, instead, the retiring partner leaves some or all of what is due to him as a loan to the partnership that will be repaid in the future.

Debit   Retiring partner's capital account

Credit Loan account

Step 4

We must now remove the goodwill from the ledger by:

Debit   Remaining partners' capital accounts in profit share ratio

Credit Goodwill account with the value of the goodwill

Example

Rob, Marc and Di have been in partnership for a number of years sharing profits in the ratio of 3:2:1.

On 1 March 20X3 Rob retired from the partnership and at that date the goodwill was valued at £60,000.

The other two partners agreed with Rob that he would be paid £20,000 of what was due to him in cash and the remainder would be a loan to the partnership.

After Rob's retirement Marc and Di are to share profits in the ratio of 2:1.

The capital account and current account balances at 1 March 20X3 were as follows:

			£
Capital accounts	–	Rob	65,000
		Marc	55,000
		Di	40,000
Current accounts	–	Rob	8,000
		Marc	5,000
		Di	2,000

Write up the partners' capital accounts to reflect the retirement of Rob.

Solution

Step 1

Transfer Rob's current account balance to his capital account.

Capital accounts

	Rob £	Marc £	Di £		Rob £	Marc £	Di £
				Bal b/d	65,000	55,000	40,000
				Current a/c	8,000		

Current accounts

	Rob £	Marc £	Di £		Rob £	Marc £	Di £
Capital a/c	8,000			Bal b/d	8,000	5,000	2,000

Step 2

Temporarily open up a goodwill account and credit the partners' capital accounts in the old profit sharing ratio.

Goodwill account

	£		£
Capital accounts	60,000		

Capital accounts

	Rob £	Marc £	Di £		Rob £	Marc £	Di £
				Bal b/d	65,000	55,000	40,000
				Current a/c	8,000		
				Goodwill	30,000	20,000	10,000

Step 3

Pay Rob off as agreed – £20,000 in cash and the remainder as a loan.

Capital accounts

	Rob £	Marc £	Di £		Rob £	Marc £	Di £
Bank	20,000			Bal b/d	65,000	55,000	40,000
Loan	83,000			Current a/c	8,000		
				Goodwill	30,000	20,000	10,000
	103,000				103,000		

Step 4

Remove the goodwill from the ledger with a credit to the goodwill account and a debit to the remaining partners' capital accounts in the new profit share ratio.

Goodwill account

	£		£
Capital accounts	60,000	Capital accounts	60,000

Capital accounts

	Rob £	Marc £	Di £		Rob £	Marc £	Di £
Bank	20,000			Bal b/d	65,000	55,000	40,000
Loan	83,000			Current a/c	8,000		
Goodwill		40,000	20,000				
Bal c/d	–	35,000	30,000	Goodwill	30,000	20,000	10,000
	103,000	75,000	50,000		103,000	75,000	50,000
				Bal b/d		35,000	30,000

You can see that Marc's capital account balance has reduced by £20,000 and that Di's has reduced by £10,000.

They have effectively been charged with the £30,000 of goodwill that has to be paid to Rob on his retirement. Consequently Marc and Di will have a greater share of profits.

 Test your understanding 5

M, N and P have been in partnership for a number of years sharing profits equally.

On 30 June 20X4 M is to retire from the partnership and thereafter N and P will share profits equally.

The value of the goodwill of the partnership is estimated to be £30,000 and M has agreed to leave the entire amount due to him on loan to the partnership.

The capital and current account balances at 30 June 20X4 are as follows:

Current accounts

	M £	N £	P £		M £	N £	P £
				Balance b/d	4,000	5,000	6,000

Write up the partners' capital accounts to reflect the retirement of M.

Capital accounts

	M £	N £	P £		M £	N £	P £
				Balance b/d	50,000	40,000	30,000
	___	___	___		___	___	___
	___	___	___		___	___	___

6 Preparing financial statements for a partnership

6.1 Statement of profit or loss

The first stage in preparing a partnership's financial statements from either a trial balance or an extended trial balance is to prepare the statement of profit or loss. This will be exactly the same as the preparation of a statement of profit or loss for a sole trader with the same types of adjustments such as depreciation expenses, closing inventory, irrecoverable and doubtful debts and accruals and prepayments

6.2 Appropriation of profit

The next stage is to take the net profit from the statement of profit or loss and prepare an appropriation account in order to split the profit between the partners in the profit share ratio to include in their current accounts.

Remember that if the profit share ratio has changed during the period, the appropriation must be done in two separate calculations.

6.3 Drawings

In the trial balance there will be account balances for each partner's drawings, these must be transferred to the partners' current accounts and the balance on each partner's current account identified.

6.4　Statement of financial position

The final stage is to prepare the statement of financial position of the partnership. The top part of the statement of financial position will be exactly the same as that for a sole trader. Only the capital section of the statement of financial position is different. Here the capital account balances and the current account balances for each partner are listed and totalled, and this total should agree with the net assets total of the top part of the statement of financial position.

🔆 Example

A, B and C are in partnership with a partnership agreement that B receives a salary of £8,000 per annum and C a salary of £12,000 per annum.

Interest on capital is allowed at 4% per annum and the profits are shared in the ratio of 2:1:1.

The list of ledger balances at the year end of 31 March 20X4 are given below:

		£
Drawings	A	43,200
	B	26,000
	C	30,200
Purchases ledger control account		56,000
Bank balance		2,800
Current accounts at 1 April 20X3	A	3,500
	B	7,000
	C	4,200
Purchases		422,800
Inventory at 1 April 20X3		63,000
Capital accounts	A	42,000
	B	32,200
	C	14,000
Sales ledger control account		75,600
Revenue		651,000
Non-current assets at cost		112,000
Accumulated depreciation at 1 April 20X3		58,900
Allowance for doubtful debts at 1 April 20X3		2,000
Expenses		95,200

You are also given the following information:

(i)　Inventory at 31 March 20X4 has been valued at £70,000.

(ii)　Depreciation for the year has yet to be provided at 20% on cost.

(iii)　An irrecoverable debt of £5,600 is to be written off and an allowance for doubtful debts is to be 2% of the remaining receivables.

(iv)　Expenses of £7,000 are to be accrued.

Task 1

Draw up are initial trial balance at 31 March 20X4

Trial balance at 31 March 20X4

		£	£
Drawings	A	43,200	
	B	26,000	
	C	30,200	
Purchases ledger control account			56,000
Bank balance		2,800	
Current accounts at 1 April 20X3	A		3,500
	B		7,000
	C		4,200
Purchases		422,800	
Capital accounts	A		42,000
	B		32,200
	C		14,000
Inventory at 1 April 20X3		63,000	
Sales ledger control account		75,600	
Sales			651,000
Non-current assets at cost		112,000	
Accumulated depreciation at 1 April 20X3			58,900
Allowance for doubtful debts at 1 April 20X3			2,000
Expenses		95,200	
		870,800	870,800

Task 2

Prepare the statement of profit or loss for the year ended 31 March 20X4.

Statement of profit or loss for the year ending 31 March 20X4

		£	£
Revenue			651,000
Less:	Cost of goods sold		
	Opening inventory	63,000	
	Purchases	422,800	
		485,800	
Less:	Closing inventory	(70,000)	
			415,800
Gross profit			235,200
Less:	Expenses (95,200 + 7,000)	102,200	
	Depreciation (20% × 112,000)	22,400	
	Irrecoverable debts	5,600	
	Allowance in doubtful debt adjustment		
	(2% × (75,600 – 5,600) – 2,000)	(600)	
Total expenses			129,600
Net profit			105,600

Task 3

Prepare the appropriation account.

Appropriation account

			£	£
Net profit				105,600
Salaries	–	B	8,000	
		C	12,000	
			———	(20,000)
Interest on capital	–	A (42,000 × 4%)	1,680	
		B (32,200 × 4%)	1,288	
		C (14,000 × 4%)	560	
			———	
				(3,528)
				———
Profit for profit share				82,072
A (82,072 × 2/4)			41,036	
B (82,072 × 1/4)			20,518	
C (82,072 × 1/4)			20,518	
			———	
				82,072
				———

Task 4

Prepare the partners current account to include salaries, interest, profit share and drawings.

Current accounts

	A	B	C		A	B	C
	£	£	£		£	£	£
Drawings	43,200	26,000	30,200	Balance b/d	3,500	7,000	4,200
				Salaries		8,000	12,000
				Interest on cap	1,680	1,288	560
Balance c/d	3,016	10,806	7,078	Profit share	41,036	20,518	20,518
	———	———	———		———	———	———
	46,216	36,806	37,278		46,216	36,806	37,278
	———	———	———		———	———	———
				Balance b/d	3,016	10,806	7,078

Task 5

Prepare the statement of financial position for the partnership at 31 March 20X4

Statement of financial position as at 31 March 20X4

	£	£	£
Non-current assets at cost			112,000
Accumulated depreciation (58,900 + 22,400)			(81,300)
			————
Carrying amount			30,700
Current assets			
Inventory		70,000	
Trade receivables	70,000		
Less: Allowance for doubtful debts	(1,400)		
	————	68,600	
Bank		2,800	
		————	
		141,400	
Current liabilities:			
Trade payables	56,000		
Accruals	7,000		
	————		
		(63,000)	
		————	
Net current assets			78,400
			————
Net assets			109,100
			————

	£	£
Capital accounts – A	42,000	
B	32,200	
C	14,000	
	————	
		88,200
Current accounts – A	3,016	
B	10,806	
C	7,078	
	————	
		20,900
		————
		109,100
		————

Test your understanding 6

The partnership of Lyle and Tate has made a net profit of £58,000 for the year ended 30 June 20X3.

The partnership agreement is that Tate receives a salary of £8,000 per annum and that the profits are split in the ratio of 3:2.

The list of statement of financial position balances at 30 June 20X3 are given below:

			£
Capital accounts	–	Lyle	75,000
		Tate	50,000
Current accounts at 1 July 20X2	–	Lyle	3,000
		Tate	2,000
Drawings	–	Lyle	28,000
		Tate	24,000
Non-current assets at cost			100,000
Accumulated depreciation at 30 June 20X3			30,000
Inventory at 30 June 20X3			44,000
Trade receivables			38,000
Bank			10,000
Trade payables			26,000

Prepare the appropriation account

Appropriation account

	£	£
Net profit		
Salary – Tate		
		———
Profit available		
		———
Profit share – Lyle		
Tate		
		———
		———

Write up and balance the partners' current accounts.

Current accounts

	Lyle £	Tate £		Lyle £	Tate £
Drawings			Balance b/d		
Balance c/d			Appropriation a/c		
	_____	_____		_____	_____
	_____	_____		_____	_____
			Balance b/d		

Prepare the statement of financial position as at 30 June 20X3.

Statement of financial position as at 30 June 20X3

	£	£
Non-current assets at cost		
Accumulated depreciation		_____
Current assets		
Inventory		
Trade Receivables		
Bank		
	_____	
Less: Trade payables		
Net current assets		
		_____
Net assets		_____
Capital accounts	Lyle	
	Tate	
		_____
Current accounts	Lyle	
	Tate	
		_____
		_____

Partnership accounts will always appear in the AAT exam but you will never have to deal with a partnership with more than three partners.

Test your understanding 7

1   What is the double entry when a partner withdraws goods from the partnership?

Debit

Credit

2   What is the double entry required to transfer a partner's drawings from the drawings account to the current account? (complete the account name in the box)

Debit

Credit

3   What is the double entry for interest on a partner's capital?

Debit

Credit

4   What is the goodwill of a partnership?

_____

_____

_____

_____

5   Is goodwill normally recorded as a permanent asset of a partnership?

No   ☐

Yes   ☐

Test your understanding 8

Low, High and Broad

Low, High and Broad are in partnership sharing profits and losses in the ratio 2:2:1 respectively. Interest is credited on partners' capital account balances at the rate of 5% per annum.

High is the firm's sales manager and for his specialised services he is to receive a salary of £800 per annum.

During the year ended 30 April 20X1 the profit for the year of the firm was £6,200 and the partners' drawings were as follows:

	£
Low	1,200
High	800
Broad	800

On 31 October 20X0 the firm agreed that Low and Broad should subscribe £1,000 each to their capital accounts.

The credit balances on the partners' accounts at 1 May 20X0 were as follows:

	Capital accounts £	Current accounts £
Low	8,000	640
High	7,000	560
Broad	6,000	480

Required:

(a) **Prepare a profit appropriation statement for the year ended 30 April 20X1.**

(b) **Prepare the partners' capital and current accounts for the year ended 30 April 20X1.**

Test your understanding 9

Curran and Edgar are in partnership as motor engineers.

The following figures were available after the preparation of the trial balance at 31 December 20X3.

Capital account (C)	£26,000
Capital account (E)	£20,000
Current account (C)	£6,100
Current account (E)	£5,200

Both current accounts showed credit balances

Drawings (C)	£16,250
Drawings (E)	£14,750

After the preparation of the statement of profit or loss, profit was determined as £42,100.

Profits are shared equally by the partners.

Task 1

Show the capital account for each partner updated to 1 January 20X4.

Task 2

Prepare the current account for each partner, balancing these off at the year end.

 Test your understanding 10

Kate and Ed have been in partnership for a number of years sharing profits and losses equally.

On 1 March 20X3 it was decided to admit Rob to the partnership and he would introduce £30,000 of additional capital by payment into the partnership bank account.

Kate and Ed had capital balances on 1 March 20X3 of £50,000 and £40,000 respectively and the goodwill of the partnership was estimated to be £35,000.

After the admission of Rob, the partnership profits are to be shared with two fifths to Kate and Ed each and one fifth to Rob.

Write up the partners' capital accounts to reflect the admission of Rob.

Test your understanding 11

Liam, Sam and Fred have been in partnership for a number of years sharing profits in the ratio of 3:2:1.

On 31 May 20X4 Liam retired from the partnership. He was due to be paid £20,000 on that date and the remainder is to remain as a loan to the partnership.

After Liam's retirement Sam and Fred are to share profits equally. The goodwill of the partnership at 31 May 20X4 was estimated to total £18,000.

The partners' capital and current account balances at 31 May 20X4 were as follows:

	£
Capital accounts	
Liam	50,000
Sam	40,000
Fred	30,000
Current accounts	
Liam	4,000
Sam	2,000
Fred	3,000

You are to write up the partners' capital accounts to reflect the retirement of Liam.

 Test your understanding 12

Wilson and Bridget are in partnership running a toyshop. They have not had a successful year and have reported a loss of £56,000 in the year ended 30 September 20X8.

Their partnership agreement states the following:

- A salary of £9,000 for Wilson and £12,000 for Bridget.

- Interest on drawings above £10,000 in the year at 5%.

- Interest on capital at 10%.

- The balance of the profits to be shared equally.

Wilson has invested £30,000 in the business and Bridget £15,000. Wilson and Bridget took £14,000 and £8,000 respectively as drawings on 1 July 20X8.

What is Wilson's share of the loss?

7 Summary

In this chapter we have dealt with all aspects of partnership accounts which are required for the exam. The AAT examination will always feature partnership accounting so this is an important area. In terms of preparing financial statements for a partnership, the preparation of the statement of profit or loss is exactly the same as that for a sole trader; therefore in this chapter we have concentrated on the areas of difference between a sole trader and a partnership.

When partners pay capital into the partnership this is recorded in the partner's individual capital account. The profit of the partnership must then be shared between the partners according to the partnership agreement. This may include salaries for some partners, interest on capital as well as the final profit share ratio. All aspects of sharing out the profit take place in the appropriation account which can take the form of a ledger account or a vertical statement. The appropriated profit is credited to the partners' current accounts and their current accounts are debited with their drawings for the period. The balances on the partners' capital accounts and current accounts are listed in the bottom part of the statement of financial position and should be equal in total to the net assets total of the top part of the statement of financial position.

You may also be required to deal with changes in the partnership. The most straightforward of these is a change in the profit share ratio during the period. This requires a separate appropriation for the period before the change according to the old profit share ratio and then for the period after the change using the new profit share ratio.

If a partner is admitted to the partnership or a partner retires then the goodwill of the partnership has to be considered. The goodwill is not recorded in the partnership books but upon a change, such as an admission or retirement, it must be brought into account to ensure that each partner is given full credit, not only for the recorded assets but also for the goodwill. The treatment is fundamentally the same for both an admission and a retirement. The goodwill account is temporarily set up as a debit (an asset) and the partners' capital accounts are credited in the old profit share ratio. The goodwill is then removed with a credit entry to the goodwill account and debits to the partners' capital accounts in the new profit share ratio.

Test your understanding answers

Test your understanding 1

Capital account – A

	£		£
Balance c/d	20,000	Balance b/d	15,000
		Bank	5,000
	20,000		20,000
		Balance b/d	20,000

Capital account – B

	£		£
Balance c/d	15,000	Balance b/d	15,000
	15,000		15,000
		Balance b/d	15,000

Current account – A

	£		£
Drawings	12,000	Balance b/d	4,000
Balance c/d	6,000	Profit	14,000
	18,000		18,000
		Balance b/d	6,000

Current account – B

	£		£
Drawings	13,000	Balance b/d	2,000
Balance c/d	3,000	Profit	14,000
	16,000		16,000
		Balance b/d	3,000

Trial balance extract

	Dr £	Cr £
Capital account – A		20,000
Capital account – B		15,000
Current account – A		6,000
Current account – B		3,000

Test your understanding 2

Appropriation account

		£	£
Net profit			120,000
Salary – Ted		20,000	
Sales commission –	Nick (2.5% × 82,400)	2,060	
	Ted (2.5% × 48,600)	1,215	
Interest on capital –	Nick (6% × 150,000)	9,000	
	Ted (6% × 100,000)	6,000	
			(38,275)
Profit available			81,725
Profit share –	Nick (81,725 × 3/5)		49,035
	Ted (81,725 × 2/5)		32,690
			81,725

Current accounts

	Nick £	Ted £		Nick £	Ted £
Balance b/d		1,000	Balance b/d	3,000	
Drawings	56,000	59,000	Salary		20,000
			Sales commission	2,060	1,215
			Interest on capital	9,000	6,000
			Profit share	49,035	32,690
Balance c/d	7,095		Balance c/d		95
	63,095	60,000		63,095	60,000
Balance b/d		95	Balance b/d	7,095	

KAPLAN PUBLISHING

Test your understanding 3

Appropriation account

1.7.X3 to 31.3.X4

		£
Profit to 31 March 20X4 (100,000 × 9/12)		75,000
		————
Profit share — Jill (75,000 × 2/5)	30,000	
Jane (75,000 × 2/5)	30,000	
Jan (75,000 × 1/5)	15,000	
	————	
		75,000
		————

1.4.X4 – 30.6.X4

		£
Profit to 30 June 20X4 (100,000 × 3/12)		25,000
Salary Jane (16,000 × 3/12)		(4,000)
		————
Profit available		21,000
		————
Profit share — Jill (21,000 × 1/3)	7,000	
Jane (21,000 × 1/3)	7,000	
Jan (21,000 × 1/3)	7,000	
	————	
		21,000
		————

Current accounts

	Jill	Jane	Jan		Jill	Jane	Jan
	£	£	£		£	£	£
Drawings	38,000	40,000	25,000	Balance b/d	3,000	2,000	1,000
				Profit share	30,000	30,000	15,000
				Salary		4,000	
Balance c/d	2,000	3,000		Profit share	7,000	7,000	7,000
				Balance c/d			2,000
	———	———	———		———	———	———
	40,000	43,000	25,000		40,000	43,000	25,000
	———	———	———		———	———	———
Balance b/d			2,000	Balance b/d	2,000	3,000	

Test your understanding 4

Capital accounts

	Karl £	Len £	Nina £		Karl £	Len £	Nina £
				Balance b/d	80,000	50,000	
Goodwill	6,000	6,000	3,000	Goodwill	10,000	5,000	
Balance c/d	84,000	49,000	32,000	Bank			35,000
	90,000	55,000	35,000		90,000	55,000	35,000
				Balance b/d	84,000	49,000	32,000

Test your understanding 5

Capital accounts

	M £	N £	P £		M £	N £	P £
Goodwill		15,000	15,000	Balance b/d	50,000	40,000	30,000
Loan	64,000			Current a/c	4,000		
Balance c/d		35,000	25,000	Goodwill	10,000	10,000	10,000
	64,000	50,000	40,000		64,000	50,000	40,000
				Balance b/d		35,000	25,000

Test your understanding 6

Appropriation account

	£	£
Net profit		58,000
Salary – Tate		(8,000)
Profit available		50,000
Profit share – Lyle (50,000 × 3/5)	30,000	
Tate (50,000 × 2/5)	20,000	
		50,000

Current accounts

	Lyle £	Tate £		Lyle £	Tate £
Drawings	28,000	24,000	Balance b/d	3,000	2,000
Balance c/d	5,000	6,000	Appropriation a/c	30,000	28,000
	33,000	30,000		33,000	30,000
			Balance b/d	5,000	6,000

Statement of financial position as at 30 June 20X3

	£	£
Non-current assets at cost		100,000
Accumulated depreciation		(30,000)
		70,000
Current assets:		
Inventory	44,000	
Trade receivables	38,000	
Bank	10,000	
	92,000	
Less: Trade payables	(26,000)	
Net current assets		66,000
Net assets		136,000
Capital accounts – Lyle		75,000
Tate		50,000
		125,000
Current accounts – Lyle	5,000	
Tate	6,000	
		11,000
		136,000

Test your understanding 7

1   Debit   Partner's current account
    Credit   Purchases

2   Debit   Partner's current account
    Credit   Partner's drawings account

3   Debit   Appropriation account
    Credit   Partners' current accounts

4   It is the excess of the value of the partnership as a whole over the value of its net assets.

5   No, it is not usually recorded as a permanent asset. It is normally accounted for, and then immediately removed from the accounting records, when accounting for the admission or retirement of a partner.

Test your understanding 8

(a)   **Profit appropriation statement – year ended 30 April 20X1:**

	Year ended 30 Apr 20X1 £	Total £
Profit for the year		6,200
Salaries		
Low	–	
High	(800)	
Broad	–	(800)
Interest on capital		
Six months to 31 Oct 20X0		
Low	(200)	
High	(175)	
Broad	(150)	(525)
Six months to 30 Apr 20X1		
Low	(225)	
High	(175)	
Broad	(175)	(575)
Profit available for distribution		4,300

Profit share		
Low	(1,720)	
High	(1,720)	
Broad	(860)	(4,300)
Balance		Nil

Summary of profit share for the year:

Low: £200 + £225 + £1,720 = £2,145

High: £800 + £175 + £175 + £1,720 = £2,870

Broad: £150 + £175 + £860 = £1,185

(b)

Capital accounts

	Low £	High £	Broad £		Low £	High £	Broad £
				Balance b/d	8,000	7,000	6,000
Balance c/d	9,000	7,000	7,000	Cash	1,000		1,000
	8,000	7,000	7,000		9,000	7,000	7,000
				Balance b/d	9,000	7,000	7,000

Current accounts

	Low £	High £	Broad £		Low £	High £	Broad £
Drawings	1,200	800	800	Balance b/d	640	560	480
Balance c/d	1,585	2,630	865	Profit apportionment	2,145	2,870	1,185
	2,785	3,430	1,665		2,785	3,430	1,665
				Balance b/d	1,585	2,630	865

Test your understanding 9

Capital account

	(C) £	(E) £		(C) £	(E) £
31 Dec Balance c/d	26,000	20,000	31 Dec Balance b/d	26,000	20,000
	26,000	20,000		26,000	20,000
			01 Jan Balance b/d	26,000	20,000

Current account

	(C) £	(E) £		(C) £	(E) £
31 Dec Drawings	16,250	14,750	Balance b/d	6,100	5,200
31 Dec Balance c/d	10,900	11,500	31 Dec Share of profit	21,050	21,050
	27,150	26,250		27,150	26,250
			01 Jan Balance b/d	10,900	11,500

Test your understanding 10

Capital accounts

	Kate £	Ed £	Rob £		Kate £	Ed £	Rob £
				Balance b/d	50,000	40,000	
Goodwill	14,000	14,000	7,000	Goodwill	17,500	17,500	
Balance c/d	53,500	43,500	23,000	Bank			30,000
	67,500	57,500	30,000		67,500	57,500	30,000

Test your understanding 11

Capital accounts

	Liam £	Sam £	Fred £		Liam £	Sam £	Fred £
				Balance b/d	50,000	40,000	30,000
				Current a/c	4,000		
Goodwill		9,000	9,000	Goodwill	9,000	6,000	3,000
Bank	20,000						
Loan	43,000						
Balance c/d		37,000	24,000				
	63,000	46,000	33,000		63,000	46,000	33,000

Test your understanding 12

	Year ended 30 Sep 20X8 £	Total £
Loss for the year		(56,000)
Salaries		
Wilson	(9,000)	
Bridget	(12,000)	(21,000)
Interest on capital		
Wilson	(3,000)	
Bridget	(1,500)	(4,500)
Interest on drawings		
Wilson (£4,000 × 5% × 3/12)	50	
Bridget	–	50
Loss available for distribution		(81,450)
Loss share		
A	40,725	
B	40,725	81,450
Balance		Nil

Wilson's total share = £9,000 + £3,000 − £50 − £40,725 = **£28,775 loss.**

Incomplete records

3

Introduction

The reconstruction of financial information from incomplete evidence is a key element of this unit when preparing accounts for a business.

There are a variety of techniques that can be used to reconstruct financial information when full accounting records are not available.

These include reconstruction of net asset totals, reconstruction of cash, bank, receivables and payables accounts and the use of mark-ups or margins in order to calculate missing accounting figures.

Each of these techniques will be considered in this chapter.

ASSESSMENT CRITERIA
Recognise circumstances where there are incomplete records (3.1)
Prepare ledger accounts, using these to estimate missing figures (3.2)
Calculate figures using mark-up and margin (3.3)
Assess the reasonableness of given figures within a particular context (3.4)

CONTENTS

1 What are incomplete records?

1.1 Introduction

So far in this text we have been considering the accounting systems of sole traders and partnerships. They have all kept full accounting records consisting of primary records and a full set of ledger accounts, leading to a trial balance from which final accounts could be prepared.

In this chapter we will be considering businesses that do not keep full accounting records – incomplete records.

1.2 Limited records

Many businesses especially those of small sole traders or partnerships will only keep the bare minimum of accounting records. These may typically consist of:

- bank statements
- files of invoices sent to customers probably marked off when paid
- files of invoices received from suppliers marked off when paid
- files of bills marked off when paid
- till rolls
- a record of non-current assets owned.

From these records it will normally be possible to piece together the information required to prepare a statement of profit or loss and a statement of financial position but a number of techniques are required. These will all be covered in this chapter.

1.3 Destroyed records

In some situations, particularly in examinations, either the whole, or part of, the accounting records have been destroyed by fire, flood, thieves or computer failure. It will then be necessary to try to piece together the picture of the business from the information that is available.

1.4 Missing figures

A further element of incomplete records is that a particular figure or balance may be missing. Typically, inventory will be destroyed in accidents and drawings will be unknown. Incomplete records techniques can be used to find the missing amount or value as a balancing figure.

1.5 Techniques

In order to deal with these situations a number of specific accounting techniques are required and these will be dealt with in this chapter. They are:

- the net assets approach (based on the accounting equation)

- the cash and bank account

- receivables and payables control accounts

- mark-ups and margins.

2 The net assets approach

2.1 Introduction

The net assets approach is used in a particular type of incomplete records situation. This is where there are no detailed records of the transactions of the business during the accounting period. This may be due to the fact that they have been destroyed or that they were never kept in the first place. The only facts that can be determined are the net assets at the start of the year, the net assets at the end of the year and some details about the capital of the business.

2.2 The accounting equation

We have come across the accounting equation in earlier chapters when dealing with the statement of financial position.

The basic accounting equation is that:

Net assets = Capital

Remember that net assets = business assets – business liabilities

This can be expanded to:

Increase in net assets = Capital introduced + profit – drawings

This is important: any increase in the net assets of the business must be due to the introduction of new capital and/or the making of profit less drawings.

2.3 Using the accounting equation

If the opening net assets of the business can be determined and also the closing net assets then the increase in net assets is the difference.

Therefore if any capital introduced is known together with any drawings made by the owner, then the profit for the period can be deduced.

Alternatively if the profit and capital introduced are known then the drawings can be found as the balancing figure.

 Example

Archibald started a business on 1 January 20X1 with £2,000. On 31 December 20X1 the position of the business was as follows:

	£
It owned	
Freehold lock–up shop, at cost	4,000
Shop fixtures and equipment, at cost	500
Inventory of goods bought for resale, at cost	10,300
Debts owing by customers	500
Cash in till	10
Cash at bank	150
It owed	
Mortgage on shop premises	3,000
Payables for goods	7,000
Accrued mortgage interest	100

Archibald had drawn £500 for personal living expenses.

The shop fixtures are to be depreciated by £50 and certain goods in inventory which had cost £300 can be sold for only £50.

No records had been maintained throughout the year.

You are required to calculate the profit earned by Archibald's business in the year ended 31 December 20X1.

Solution

This sort of question is answered by calculating the net assets at the year-end as follows:

Net assets at 31 December 20X1

	Cost £	Depreciation £	CV £
Non-current assets			
Freehold shop	4,000	–	4,000
Fixtures and fittings	500	50	450
	4,500	50	4,450

Current assets		
Inventory at lower of cost and net realisable value (10,300 – 300 + 50)		10,050
Trade receivables		500
Cash and bank balances (150 + 10)		160
		10,710
Current liabilities		
Trade payables	7,000	
Mortgage interest	100	
		(7,100)
		3,610
		8,060
Mortgage		(3,000)
Net assets		5,060

The profit is now calculated from the accounting equation.

Note that the opening net assets will be the cash paid into the bank when the business was started on 1 January 20X1.

Change in net assets during the year = Profit plus capital introduced in year less drawings

£5,060 – 2,000   = Profit + Nil – 500

£3,060   = Profit – 500

Therefore, profit = £3,560

Archibald's statement of financial position is made up of the above together with the bottom half which can be established after calculating the profit, i.e.

	£
Capital	2,000
Profit (balancing figure)	3,560
	5,560
Drawings	(500)
	5,060

As you can see, the 'incomplete records' part of the question is concerned with just one figure. The question is really about the preparation of the statement of financial position.

Test your understanding 1

The net assets of a business at the start of the year were £14,600. At the end of the year the net assets were £17,300. During the year the owner had paid in £2,000 of additional long term capital and withdrew £10,000 from the business for living expenses.

What is the profit of the business?

3 Cash and bank account

3.1 Introduction

In this section we must be quite clear about the distinction between cash and bank accounts.

 Definition

Cash is the amount of notes and coins in a till or in the petty cash box.

 Definition

The bank account is the amount held in the current account or cheque account of the business.

If the opening and closing balances of cash and bank are known together with most of the movements in and out, then, if there is only one missing figure this can be found as the balancing figure.

3.2 Cash account

When dealing with incomplete records a cash account deals literally with cash either from the petty cash box or more usually from the till in a small retail business. If the opening balance and the closing balance of cash is known then provided there is only one missing figure this can be determined from the summarised cash account.

Example

Henry's sales are all for cash. During the year he:

- banked £50,000

- paid wages of £5,000 out of the till, and

- paid expenses in cash of £10,000.

There were no opening or closing cash balances.

What were Henry's sales?

Solution

Working cash account

	£		£
Cash sales (bal fig)	65,000	Bank	50,000
		Wages	5,000
		Expenses	10,000
	———		———
	65,000		65,000
	———		———

The rationale is that if £65,000 of cash was taken out of the till for various purposes then £65,000 must have come in.

 Test your understanding 2

Henrietta runs a milliner's shop making all her sales for cash. You ascertain the following information:

	£
Cash in the till at the beginning of the year	50
Cash in the till at the end of the year	75
Bingo winnings put into the till	500
Bankings	15,000
Cash wages	1,000
Cash expenses	5,000

Complete the ledger account below to establish Henrietta's sales during the year.

Working cash account

	£		£

3.3 Bank account

The same ideas can be applied to the bank account – if the opening and closing balances and all of the transactions except one are known then this missing figure can be found. In practice this may not be required though as bank statements should show all the necessary details.

Note that the double entry for bankings is

Dr   Bank account

Cr   Cash account

 Example

Henry writes cheques only for his own use. He knows that his bankings were £50,000.

The opening and closing bank balances were £10,000 and £40,000 respectively. What were his drawings?

Solution

Working bank account

	£		£
Balance b/d	10,000	Drawings (bal fig)	20,000
Bankings	50,000	Balance c/d	40,000
	————		————
	60,000		60,000
	————		————
Balance b/d	40,000		

The bankings are the amount paid out of the till and into the bank account. Therefore they must be a debit entry in the bank account.

KAPLAN PUBLISHING

3.4 Combined cash and bank account

In examinations it is often easier to combine the cash and bank accounts into one ledger account with a column for cash and a column for bank.

In the case of Henry this would be written as:

Working cash and bank account						
	Cash £	Bank £			Cash £	Bank £
Balance b/d		10,000	Drawings (bal fig)			20,000
Bankings		50,000	Bankings		50,000	
Cash sales (bal fig)	65,000		Wages		5,000	
			Expenses		10,000	
			Balance c/d			40,000
	_____	_____			_____	_____
	65,000	60,000			65,000	60,000
	_____	_____			_____	_____

The key figure here is the bankings. If the bankings were paid into the bank account then they must have come out of the till or cash account.

In examinations you may only be given the bankings figure from the bank statement – this will show the amount paid into the bank account. You must then ensure that you make this entry not only as a debit in the bank column but also as a credit in the cash column.

4 Sales ledger control account and purchase ledger control account

4.1 Introduction

In many incomplete records situations you will find that the figures for sales and purchases are missing.

A technique for finding these missing figures is to recreate the receivables and payables accounts in order to find the missing figures as balancing figures.

The sales ledger control account and the purchase ledger control account are used to find the missing figures.

4.2 Sales ledger control account

Firstly a reminder of what is likely to be in a sales ledger control account is below:

Sales ledger control account

	£		£
Opening balance	X	Receipts from customers	X
Sales (per sales day book)	X	Sales returns	X
		Irrecoverable debts	X
		Discounts allowed	X
		Contra with PLCA	X
		Closing balance	X
	X		X

If the opening and closing receivables are known, together with the receipts from customers, contras and details of any irrecoverable debts then the sales figure can be found as the balancing figure.

 Example

A business has receivables at the start of the year of £4,220 and at the end of the year receivables of £4,870, after accounting for the contra with the PLCA as noted below.

During the year customers paid a total of £156,350 and one debt of £1,000 was irrecoverable. In addition, an agreed amount of £2,000 due from a credit customer was offset against the PLCA amount due to that same customer who also makes supplies to the business on credit.

What were the sales for the year?

Solution

Sales ledger control account

	£		£
Opening balance	4,220	Receipts from customers	156,350
		Irrecoverable debt written off	1,000
		Contra with PLCA	2,000
Sales (bal fig)	160,000	Closing balance	4,870
	164,220		164,220

The sales figure of £160,000 can be deduced from this account as the balancing figure.

4.3 Purchase ledger control account

The purchase ledger control account works in the same way as a potential working for finding the purchases figure.

Purchase ledger control account

	£		£
Payments to suppliers	X	Opening balance	X
Discount received	X	Purchases	X
Purchase returns	X		
Contra with SLCA	X		
Closing balance	X		
	—		—
	X		X
	—		—

Example

Dominic paid his payables £5,000 during a period.

At the beginning of the period he owed £1,500 and at the end he owed £750, after accounting for the contra account entry as explained below. Dominic also agreed to contra an amount of £250 which was owed to a supplier who is also a credit customer of Dominic. What were his purchases for the period?

Solution

Purchase ledger control account

	£		£
Cash	5,000	Balance b/d	1,500
Contra with SLCA	250	Purchases (bal fig)	4,500
Balance c/d	750		
	———		———
	6,000		6,000
	———		———
		Balance b/d	750

4.4 Cash, bank, receivables and payables

In many incomplete records questions you will need to combine the techniques learnt so far.

You may need to use the cash and bank account in order to determine the receipts from customers and then transfer this amount to the sales ledger control account in order to find the sales figure.

Example

Andrea does not keep a full set of accounting records but she has been able to provide you with some information about her opening and closing balances for the year ended 31 December 20X1.

	1 January 20X1 £	31 December 20X1 £
Inventory	5,227	4,892
Trade receivables	6,387	7,221
Trade payables	3,859	4,209
Bank	1,448	1,382
Cash	450	300

Andrea tells you that the trade receivables balances and the trade payables balances at 31 December 20X1 are stated after accounting for a contra entry of £400 to offset an agreed amount due from another business which also supplies goods to her.

You have also been provided with a summary of Andrea's payments out of her bank account:

	£
Payments to trade payables	48,906
Purchase of new car	12,000
Payment of expenses	14,559

Andrea also tells you that she has taken £100 per week out of the till in cash in order to meet her own expenses.

Calculate sales, purchases, cost of goods sold and gross profit for Andrea for the year ended 31 December 20X1.

Solution

Step 1

Open up ledger accounts for cash and bank, receivables and payables and enter the opening and closing balances given.

Cash and bank

	Cash £	Bank £		Cash £	Bank £
Opening balance	450	1,448	Closing balance	300	1,382

Sales ledger control account

	£		£
Opening balance	6,387	Closing balance	7,221

Purchase ledger control account

	£		£
Closing balance	4,209	Opening balance	3,859

Step 2

Enter the payments from the bank account in the credit column of the bank account and complete the double entry for the payable's payment.

Cash and bank

	Cash £	Bank £		Cash £	Bank £
Opening balance	450	1,448	Payables		48,906
			Car		12,000
			Expenses		14,559
			Closing balance	300	1,382

Purchase ledger control account

	£		£
Bank	48,906	Opening balance	3,859
Closing balance	4,209		

Step 3

Find the balancing figure in the bank account as this is the amount of money paid into the bank in the period. If it was paid into the bank it must have come out of the till therefore enter the same figure as a credit in the cash account.

Cash and bank

	Cash	Bank		Cash	Bank
Opening balance	450	1,448	Payables		48,906
Bankings (bal fig)		75,399	Car		12,000
			Expenses		14,559
			Bankings	75,399	
			Closing balance	300	1,382
		76,847			76,847

Step 4

Enter the drawings into the cash account (assume a 52-week year unless told otherwise).

Cash and bank

	Cash £	Bank £		Cash £	Bank £
Opening balance	450	1,448	Payables		48,906
Bankings (bal fig)		75,399	Car		12,000
			Expenses		14,559
			Bankings	75,399	
			Drawings	5,200	
			Closing balance	300	1,382
		76,847			76,847

Step 5

Balance the cash account – the missing figure is the amount of receipts from customers – this is a debit in the cash account and a credit in the sales ledger control account.

Cash and bank

	Cash £	Bank £		Cash £	Bank £
Opening balance	450	1,448	Payables		48,906
Bankings (bal fig)		75,399	Car		12,000
			Expenses		14,559
			Bankings	75,399	
			Drawings	5,200	
Receipts – receivables (bal fig)	80,449		Closing balance	300	1,382
	80,899	76,847		80,899	76,847

Sales ledger control account

	£		£
Opening balance	6,387	Receipts from customers	80,449
		Closing balance	7,221

The receipts figure of £80,449 is not technically all from receivables since some may be for cash sales; however as the sales ledger control account is only a working account designed to find the total sales this distinction is unimportant.

Step 6

Find the sales and purchases figures as the missing figures in the receivables and payables account.

Sales ledger control account

	£		£
Opening balance	6,387	Receipts from customers	80,449
		Contra with PLCA	400
Sales (bal fig)	81,683	Closing balance	7,221
	88,070		88,070

Purchase ledger control account

	£		£
Bank	48,906	Opening balance	3,859
Contra with SLCA	400		
Closing balance	4,209	Purchases (bal fig)	49,656
	53,515		53,515

Step 7

Prepare the Trading account

	£	£
Revenue		81,683
Less: cost of goods sold		
Opening inventory	5,227	
Purchases	49,656	
	54,883	
Less: closing inventory	(4,892)	
		(49,991)
Gross profit		31,692

In this example we dealt with all four accounts – cash, bank, receivables and payables – simultaneously in order to show how the double entry works between the four working accounts.

However in examinations you will be prompted to work through the situation step by step. So, this same example might be approached in the examination as follows.

Task 1

Calculate the amount of cash received from customers from sales.

This will come from the cash and bank account workings

Cash and bank

	Cash £	Bank £		Cash £	Bank £
Opening balance	450	1,448	Payables		48,906
Bankings (bal fig)		75,399	Car		12,000
			Expenses		14,559
			Bankings	75,399	
			Drawings	5,200	
Receipts – receivables (bal fig)	80,449		Closing balance	300	1,382
	80,899	76,847		80,899	76,847

Cash from customers for sales = £80,449

Task 2

Determine the sales for the period.

This will come from the working sales ledger control account.

Sales ledger control account

	£		£
Opening balance	6,387	Receipts from customers	80,449
		Contra with PLCA	400
Sales (bal fig)	81,683	Closing balance	7,221
	88,070		88,070

Sales = £81,683

Task 3

Determine the purchases for the period.

This will come from the working purchase ledger control account.

Purchase ledger control account

	£		£
Bank	48,906	Opening balance	3,859
Contra with SLCA	400		
Closing balance	4,209	Purchases (bal fig)	49,656
	53,515		53,515

Purchases = £49,656

Task 4

Calculate the gross profit for the period.

This will come from the statement of profit or loss.

	£	£
Revenue		81,683
Less: cost of goods sold		
Opening inventory	5,227	
Purchases	49,656	
	———	
	54,883	
Less: closing inventory	(4,892)	
	———	(49,991)
		———
Gross profit		31,692
		———

Gross profit = £31,692

5 Margins and mark-ups

5.1 Introduction

The final technique that you may be required to use is that of dealing with margins and mark-ups. This is often useful when dealing with the records of a retailer and is a useful method of reconstructing missing figures.

5.2 Cost structure

The key to dealing with mark-ups and margins is in setting up the cost structure of the sales of an organisation from the information given in the question.

Definition

A cost structure is the relationship between the selling price of goods, their cost and the gross profit earned in percentage terms.

Example

An item is sold for £150 and it originally cost £100. We need to set up the cost structure for this sale.

Solution

	£
Revenue	150
Cost of goods sold	100
Gross profit	50

The cost structure, in percentage terms, can be set up in one of two ways.

(i) Assume that cost of goods sold represents 100% therefore the cost structure would be:

	£	%
Revenue	150	150
Cost of goods sold	100	100
Gross profit	50	50

We can now say that this sale gives a gross profit percentage of 50% on cost of goods sold.

(ii) Assume that revenue represents 100% therefore the cost structure would be:

	£	%
Revenue	150	100
Cost of goods sold	100	$66^2/_3$
Gross profit	50	$33^1/_3$

We can now say that this sale gives a gross profit percentage of $33^1/_3$% on sales.

5.3 The difference between a mark-up and a margin

If it is cost of goods sold that is 100% then this is known as a mark-up on cost. Therefore in the previous example the sale would be described as having a mark-up on cost of 50%.

If it is revenue that is 100% then this is known as a sales margin. In the previous example the sale would be described as having a gross profit margin of $33^{1}/_{3}\%$.

 Example

Calculate the cost of goods which have been sold for £1,200 on which a gross profit margin of 25% has been achieved.

Solution

Step 1

Work out the cost structure.

The phrase 'gross profit margin' means 'gross profit on sales'. Following the rule above we therefore make revenue equal to 100%. We know the gross profit is 25%; therefore the cost of goods sold must be 75%.

	%
Revenue	100
Less: cost of goods sold	75
	___
Gross profit	25
	___

Step 2

Work out the missing figure, in this case 'cost of goods sold'.

	£	%
Revenue	1,200	100
Cost of goods sold	?	75
	___	___
Gross profit	?	25
	___	___

$$\text{Cost of goods sold} = 75\% \text{ of revenue}$$

$$= \frac{75}{100} \times 1,200 = £900$$

Therefore gross profit = £300 (£1,200 − £900)

Example

Calculate the cost of goods which have been sold for £1,200 on which a mark-up on cost of goods sold of 25% has been achieved.

Solution

Step 1

The cost structure

The fact that the gross profit here is on cost of goods sold rather than sales as above makes all the difference. When we construct the 'cost structure', cost of goods sold will be 100%; gross profit will be 25%, so that revenue must be 125%.

In other words:

	%
Revenue	125
Less: cost of goods sold	100
	____
Gross profit	25
	____

Step 2

Calculate the missing figure, again the cost of goods sold

	£	%
Revenue	1,200	125
Cost of goods sold	?	100
	____	____
Gross profit	?	25
	____	____

Cost of goods sold = $\dfrac{100}{125}$ of revenue

$= \dfrac{100}{125} \times 1,200 = £960$

Remember the rule – whatever the margin or mark-up is 'on' or 'of' must be 100%.

- If there is a margin on sales price then revenues are 100%.

- If there is a mark-up on cost then cost of goods sold are 100%.

Test your understanding 3

(a) Mark-up on cost of goods sold = 10%

Revenues were £6,160

Cost of goods sold =

(b) Gross profit on revenues = 20%

Cost of goods sold was £20,000

Revenues =

(c) Mark-up on cost of goods sold = 33%

Cost of goods sold was £15,000

Revenues =

(d) Gross profit on revenues = 25%

Cost of goods sold was £13,200

Revenues =

(e) Revenues were £20,000

Cost of goods sold was £16,000

Gross profit on revenues as a % =

Gross profit on cost of goods sold as a % =

6 Margins and mark-ups and incomplete records

6.1 Introduction

We will now look at how mark-ups and margins can be used in incomplete records questions. They can be a great help in finding missing revenue and cost of goods sold figures but a little practice is required in using them.

6.2 Calculating revenues

In a question if you have enough information to calculate cost of goods sold and you are given some information about the cost structure of the revenues then you will be able to calculate revenue.

In examination questions if the percentage mark-up or margin is given then you will need to use it – do not try to answer the question without using it as you will get the answer wrong!

Example

A business has purchases of £18,000 and opening and closing inventory of £2,000 and £4,000 respectively. The gross profit margin is always 25%.

What are the revenues for the period?

Solution

Step 1

Cost structure

As it is a gross profit margin this is a margin 'on' revenue and therefore revenues are 100%

	%
Revenue	100
Cost of goods sold	75
Gross profit	25

Step 2

Calculate cost of goods sold

	£
Opening inventory	2,000
Purchases	18,000
	20,000
Less: closing inventory	(4,000)
	16,000

Step 3

Determine the revenue figure

$$£16,000 \times \frac{100}{75} = £21,333$$

Test your understanding 4

You are given the following information relating to Clarence's business for the year ended 31 December 20X3.

Cash paid to trade payables was £9,000. Other assets and liabilities were:

	1 January £	31 December £
Payables	2,100	2,600
Inventory	1,800	1,600

Mark-up on cost of goods sold 20%

Task 1

Calculate the purchases for the year.

Task 2

Calculate the cost of goods sold for the year.

Task 3

Calculate the revenues for the year.

6.3 Calculating cost of goods sold, purchases or closing inventory

If you know the figure for revenue and you know about the cost structure then it is possible to find the total for cost of goods sold and then deduce any missing figures such as purchases or closing inventory.

Example

A business had made sales in the month of £25,000. The business sells its goods at a mark-up of 20%. The opening inventory was £2,000 and the closing inventory was £3,000.

What were the purchases for the period?

Solution

Step 1

Cost structure

	%
Revenue	120
Cost of goods sold	100
Gross profit	20

Step 2

Determine cost of goods sold using the cost structure.

$$\text{Cost of goods sold} = £25,000 \times \frac{100}{120}$$

$$= £20,833$$

Step 3

Reconstruct cost of goods sold to find purchases

	£
Opening inventory	2,000
Purchases (bal fig)	21,833
	23,833
Less: closing inventory	(3,000)
Cost of goods sold	20,833

7 Examination style questions

7.1 Introduction

So far we have studied the techniques that you have to use to deal with incomplete records questions in the exam. Although the examiner may ask any style of question, the examiner tends to ask questions in a particular way – leading you through the question a bit at a time and telling you what you have to calculate next. We shall now see how these questions might appear in the exam.

 Example

John is a sole trader and prepares his accounts to 30 September 20X8. The summary of his bank account is as follows.

	£		£
Balance b/d 1 Oct 20X7	15,000	Stationery	2,400
Receipts from receivables	74,865	General expenses	4,300
		Rent	4,500
		Payments to suppliers	27,000
		Drawings	24,000
		Balance at 30 Sept 20X8	27,665
	89,865		**89,865**

Receivables at 1 October 20X7 were 24,000 and at 30 September 20X8 were 30,000.

Payables at 1 October 20X7 were 17,500 and at 30 September 20X8 were 23,000.

Rent was paid at £1,500 per quarter, and the rent had not been paid for the final quarter to 30 September 20X8.

During September 20X8 a payment of £300 was made for electricity which covered the period 1 August 20X8 to 31 October 20X8. Electricity is included in general expenses.

Task 1

Calculate the capital at 1 October 20X7.

Task 2

Prepare the sales ledger control account for the year ended 30 September 20X8, showing credit sales as the balancing figure.

Sales ledger control account

	£		£

Task 3

Prepare the purchases ledger control account for the year ended 30 September 20X8, showing credit purchases as the balancing figure.

Purchases ledger control account

	£		£

Task 4

Prepare the rent account for the year ended 30 September 20X8.

Rent account

	£		£

Task 5

Prepare the general expenses account for the year ended 30 September 20X8.

General expenses account

	£		£

Task 6

Prepare a trial balance at 30 September 20X8

Solution

Task 1

Capital at 1 October 20X7 = net assets at 1 October 20X7

Net assets at 1 October 20X7:	£
Bank	15,000
Receivables	24,000
Payables	(17,500)
	———
Net assets	21,500 = capital at 1 October 20X7
	———

Tutorial note. Remember that capital equals net assets. You therefore have to list all the assets and liabilities at the start of the year to find the net assets and therefore the capital.

Task 2

Sales ledger control account

	£		£
Balance b/d 1 Oct 20X7	24,000	Cash from receivables	74,865
Credit sales (bal fig)	80,865	Balance c/d 30 Sept 20X8	30,000
	———		———
	104,865		104,865
	———		———

Task 3

Purchases ledger control account

	£		£
Paid to payables	27,000	Balance b/d 1 Oct 20X7	17,500
Balance c/d 30 Sept 20X8	23,000	Purchases (bal fig)	32,500
	———		———
	50,000		50,000
	———		———

Task 4

Rent account

	£		£
Cash paid	4,500	Profit or loss	6,000
Balance c/d	1,500		
	———		———
	6,000		6,000
	———		———

Tutorial note. The £1,500 rent that has not been paid for the final quarter is an accrual – it is brought down into the next period as a credit balance as it is money owed by the business.

Task 5

General expenses account

	£		£
Cash paid	4,300	Profit or loss	4,200
		Balance c/d (1/3 × £300)	100
	———		———
	4,300		4,300
	———		———

Tutorial note. Of the £300 paid in September 20X8, £100 is for the month of October 20X8 – it is therefore a prepayment and is carried forward as an asset – a debit balance

Task 6

Trial balance as at 30 September 20X8

	£	£
Capital at 1 October 20X7		21,500
Bank	27,665	
Revenue		80,865
Sales ledger control a/c	30,000	
Purchases	32,500	
Purchases ledger control a/c		23,000
Accrual – rent		1,500
Prepayment – general expenses	100	
Stationery	2,400	
Rent (P&L)	6,000	
General expenses (P&L)	4,200	
Drawings	24,000	
	———	———
	126,865	126,865
	———	———

7.2 Another example

In many examination questions you will be required to use the incomplete records techniques to determine missing figures. We have already looked at finding revenue, cost of goods sold, purchases and closing or opening inventory. The final common missing figure is that of the owner's drawings.

Often the owner of a business will not keep a record of exactly how much has been taken out of the business especially if money tends to be taken directly from the till.

In examination questions if you are told that the owner's drawings were, for example, approximately £35 each week then this figure can be used as the actual drawings figure.

However if the question states that drawings were between £25 and £45 per week you cannot take an average figure; you must use incomplete records techniques to find the drawings figure as the balancing figure.

 Example

Simone runs a television and video shop.

All purchases are made on credit.

Sales are a mixture of cash and credit.

For the year ended 31 December 20X8, the opening and closing payables, receivables and inventory were:

	1.1.X8	21.12.X8
	£	£
Payables	11,000	11,500
Receivables	12,000	11,800
Inventory	7,000	10,000

Her mark-up is 20% on cost.

The payments for purchases are posted to the bank account and the purchase ledger control account.

All cash and cheques are posted to the cash account and sales ledger control account. Surplus cash and cheques are then paid into the bank.

A summary of her business bank account for the year ended 31 December 20X8 is as follows.

Bank account

	£		£
Balance b/d 1/1/X8	12,500	Payments to suppliers	114,000
Cash banked	121,000	Rent and rates	10,000
		Other expenses	4,000
		Balance c/d 31.12.X8	5,500
	133,500		133,500

The opening and closing cash balances were:

1/1/X8	31/12/X8
£120	£150

Cash was used to pay for petrol costing £400 and stationery costing £200. She also drew money out of the till for her personal use, but she has not kept a record of the amounts drawn.

Task 1

Prepare the purchase ledger control account

	£		£

Task 2

Calculate the cost of goods sold using the following proforma

	£
Opening inventory	
Purchases	
	———
Closing inventory	
	———
Cost of goods sold	
	———

Task 3

Calculate revenue for the year using the following proforma and the details of the mark up given in the question.

	£	%
Revenue		
Cost of goods sold		
	———	
Gross profit		
	———	

Task 4

Prepare the sales ledger control account to find the cash received from receivables during the year

	£		£

Task 5

Complete the cash account given below where drawings will be the balancing figure

Cash account

	£		£
Balance b/d		Petrol	
Receipts – receivables		Stationery	
		Bankings – to bank a/c	
		Drawings	
		Balance c/d	

Solution

Task 1

Calculation of purchases

Purchase ledger control account

	£		£
Bank account	114,000	Balance b/d	11,000
Balance c/d	11,500	Purchases (bal fig)	114,500
	————		————
	125,500		125,500
	————		————

Task 2

Calculation of cost of goods sold

	£
Opening inventory	7,000
Purchases (Task 1)	114,500
	————
	121,500
Closing inventory	(10,000)
	————
	111,500
	————

Task 3

Calculation of sales

	£	%
Revenue ($\frac{120}{100}$ × 111,500)	133,800	120
Cost of goods sold (Task 2)	111,500	100
Gross profit	22,300	20

Task 4

Sales ledger control account

	£		£
Balance b/d	12,000	Receipts (bal fig)	134,000
Revenue (Task 3)	133,800	Balance c/d	11,800
	145,800		145,800

Task 5

Drawings

Cash account

	£		£
Balance b/d	120	Petrol	400
Receipts – receivables	134,000	Stationery	200
		Bankings	121,000
		Drawings (bal fig)	12,370
		Balance c/d	150
	134,120		134,120

Take care with the order in which you work.

- As a mark-up is given you will need to use it – you have enough information to determine purchases and cost of goods sold therefore use the mark-up to calculate revenue.

- Make sure that you enter these sales into the sales ledger control account on the debit side – even though some are for cash rather than on credit they should all be entered into the receivables account as you are only using it as a vehicle for calculating the total revenue.

- Once sales have been entered into the receivables account the only missing figure is the cash received – this should be then entered into the cash account as a debit.

- Finally once all of the cash payments are entered as credits the balancing figure on the credit side of the cash account will be the drawings.

 Test your understanding 5

Ignatius owns a small wholesale business and has come to you for assistance in the preparation of his accounts for the year ended 31 December 20X4.

For the year ended 31 December 20X4 no proper accounting records have been kept, but you establish the following information:

(1) A summary of Ignatius's bank statements for the year to 31 December 20X4 is as follows:

	£		£
Opening balance	1,870	Payments to suppliers	59,660
Receipts from credit customers	12,525	Rent – one year	4,000
Cash banked	59,000	Rates – year beginning 1.4.X4	2,000
		Other administration costs	1,335
		Selling costs	1,940
		Equipment – bought 1.1.X4	800
			69,735
		Closing balance	3,660
	73,395		73,395

(2) Credit sales for the year, as shown by a summary of copy invoices, totalled £12,760.

(3) No record has been kept by Ignatius of cash sales or his personal drawings, in cash. It is apparent, however, that all sales are on the basis of a $33^1/_3$% mark-up on cost.

(4) Apart from drawings, cash payments during the year have been:

	£
Payments to suppliers	755
Sundry expenses	155
Wages	3,055

The balance of cash in hand at 31 December 20X4 is estimated at £20, and it is known that £12 was in hand at the beginning of the year.

(5) At the year-end, closing inventory, valued at cost, was £5,375 (31 December 20X3 £4,570) and payables for goods bought for resale amounted to £4,655.

(6) At 31 December 20X3 payables for goods bought for resale amounted to 3,845.

Task 1

Calculate the purchases for the year

Purchase ledger control account

	£		£
	_____		_____
	_____		_____

Task 2

Calculate the cost of goods sold for the year

	£
Opening inventory 1.1.X4	
Purchases	
	_____
Inventory 31.12.X4	
	_____
Cost of goods sold	
	_____

Task 3

Calculate total revenue for the year

Revenue = (workings)

Cost structure

Cost of goods sold =

Mark-up   =

Therefore revenue =

Task 4

Calculate the cash sales for the year

$$£$$

_____

Cash sales

_____

Task 5

Prepare calculations to determine the owner's drawings for the year.

Enter the cash sales in the cash account. This will give drawings as a balancing figure. The cash account is reproduced here.

Cash account		
£		£
_____		_____
_____		_____

Test your understanding 6

1   According to the accounting equation, what is an increase in net assets equal to? (Write your answer below.)

2   What is the double entry for bankings from the cash till to the bank account? (Circle as appropriate.)

    Debit   **Revenue account / Bank account**

    Credit   **Cash account / Takings account**

3   The opening and closing receivables for a business were £1,000 and £1,500 and receipts from customers totalled £17,500. What were revenues? (Circle as appropriate.)

    Revenues are: **£17,500 / £17,000 / £18,000**

4   The opening and closing payables for a business were £800 and £1,200 with payments to suppliers totalling £12,200. What is the purchases figure? (Circle as appropriate.)

    Purchases are: **£12,600 / £12,200 / £11,800**

5   Goods costing £2,000 were sold at a mark up of 20%. What was the selling price? (Circle as appropriate.)

    Selling price is: **£2,500 / £2,400**

6   Goods costing £2,000 were sold with a margin of 20%. What was the selling price? (Circle as appropriate.)

    Selling price is: **£2,500 / £2,400**

7   Revenues were £24,000 and were at a margin of 25%. What is the figure for cost of goods sold? (Circle as appropriate.)

    Cost of goods sold is: **£18,000 / £6,000**

8   Revenues were £24,000 and were at a mark up of 25%. What is the figure for cost of goods sold? (Circle as appropriate.)

Cost of goods sold is   **£18,000 / £19,200**

9   Revenues for a business were £100,000 achieved at a margin of 40%. Opening inventory was £7,000 and purchases were £58,000. What is the figure for closing inventory? (Complete the proforma.)

	£	£
Revenues		
Less cost of goods sold		
Opening inventory		
Purchases		
Less closing inventory		
Gross profit		

10 Revenues for a business were £80,000 and they were sold at a mark up of 25%. Opening and closing inventory was £10,000 and £8,000 respectively. What is the purchase total? (Complete the pro forma.)

	£	£
Revenues		
Less cost of goods sold		
Opening inventory		
Purchases		
Less closing inventory		
Gross profit		

Test your understanding 7

You work as a senior for a self-employed 'Licensed Accounting Technician' and Peter Ryan, the proprietor of a local shop trading in 'home brew products', is one of your clients.

The business trades under the name of Brew-By-Us.

You have been provided with the following information:

Balances as at:	31 May X0 £	31 May X1 £
Trade receivables	2,000	1,800
Trade payables	1,200	1,500
Inventory	6,000	8,000

All the business's sales and purchases are on a credit basis.

All payments for expenses have been made by cheque.

A summary of the bank transactions for the year ended 31 May 20X1 is as follows:

	£
Balance b/d	(1,015) overdrawn
Receipts	
Loan receipt	4,000
Receipts from receivables	45,000
	49,000
Wages	3,850
Advertising	750
Payments to payables	36,200
Heat and light	1,060
Shop fixtures	2,000
Insurance	400
Rent and rates	5,200
Drawings	200
Bank charges	55
Stationery	200
	49,915
Balance 31 May 20X1	(1,930) overdrawn

Additional information for the year ended 31 May 20X1 is provided below:

- Discounts allowed to customers totalled £2,750 for the year.

- The business returned £1,280 of goods to their suppliers during the year.

- Capital at 31st May 20X0 was £5,785 and Peter did not invest any further capital during the year.

- Depreciation is to be charged on the shop fixtures purchased during the year. Fixtures are depreciated at 15% using the straight line method. A full year's depreciation is to be charged in the year of acquisition.

Required:

(a) Prepare the sales ledger control account to determine the sales for the period.

(b) Prepare the purchase ledger control account to determine the purchases for the period.

(c) Prepare a statement of profit or loss for the year ended 31 May 20X1, and a statement of financial position at that date.

Test your understanding 8

Diane Kelly has been employed for several years supplying cleaning materials to schools, restaurants, public houses and industrial units.

She operates an incomplete system of accounting records for her business, from which the following information is available.

1   Assets and liabilities

	1 June 20X0 £	31 May 20X1 £
Warehouse fittings (CV)	8,000	?
Van (at cost)	–	6,500
Inventory	10,000	16,000
Trade receivables	16,000	19,000
Trade payables	15,000	20,000
Rates prepaid	1,200	1,600
Accruals		
Telephone	400	500
Heat and light	300	500

2 **Bank account summary for the year**

	£	£
Balance at 1 June 20X0		9,800
Receipts		
Receivables	79,000	
Cash sales banked	7,700	
Proceeds of sale of caravan	2,500	89,200
Payments		
Payables	70,000	
Purchase of van	6,500	
Heat and light	1,800	
Office expenses	2,600	
Rent and rates	4,200	
Telephone	1,200	
Wages	9,800	
Van expenses	1,200	
Insurance	800	98,100
Balance at 31 May X1		900

Notes

- The caravan was Diane's own personal property.

- All non-current assets are depreciated on the diminishing balance basis; a rate of 20% should be applied.

- The van was acquired on 1 June 20X0.

- During the year cash discounts of £1,100 had been allowed and £1,800 had been received.

- Diane paid sundry office expenses of £420 and used £15,600 for personal reasons – both amounts had been taken from the proceeds of cash sales.

- All the remaining cash had been banked.

Required:

(a) Determine the sales for the year.

(b) Determine the purchases for the year.

(c) Show accounts for rates, telephone and heat and light to determine the charge for the year.

(d) Prepare the statement of profit or loss for the year ended 31 May 20X1 and a statement of financial position at that date.

Test your understanding 9

(a) A business marks up its goods by 60%. Revenues are £200,000 for the year. What is the gross profit?

(b) A business makes a 30% margin on its sales. Opening inventory is £40,000, closing inventory is £10,000 and purchases are £180,000. What is the amount for revenue?

 Test your understanding 10

Data

A friend of Donald Johnson, Sheena Gordon, has been trading for just over 12 months as a dressmaker.

She has kept no accounting records at all, and she is worried that she may need professional help to sort out her financial position.

Knowing that Donald Johnson runs a successful business, Sheena Gordon approached him for advice. He recommended that you, his bookkeeper, should help Sheena Gordon.

You meet with Sheena Gordon and discuss the information that you require her to give you.

Sometime later, you receive a letter from Sheena Gordon providing you with the information that you requested, as follows:

(a) She started her business on 1 October 20X2. She opened a business bank account and paid in £5,000 of her savings.

(b) During October she bought the equipment and the inventory that she needed. The equipment cost £4,000 and the inventory of materials cost £1,800. All of this was paid for out of the business bank account.

(c)   A summary of the business bank account for the 12 months ended 30 September 20X3 showed the following:

Bank

	£		£
Capital	5,000	Equipment	4,000
Cash banked	27,000	Purchases	1,800
		Purchases of materials	18,450
		General expenses	870
		Drawings	6,200
		Balance c/d	680
	32,000		32,000

(d)   All of the sales are on a cash basis. Some of the cash is paid into the bank account while the rest is used for cash expenses. She has no idea what the total value of her sales is for the year, but she knows that from her cash received she has spent £3,800 on materials and £490 on general expenses. She took the rest of the cash not banked for her private drawings. She also keeps a cash float of £100.

(e)   The gross profit margin on all sales is 50%.

(f)   She estimates that all the equipment should last for five years. You therefore agree to depreciate it using the straight line method.

(g)   On 30 September 20X3, the payables for materials amounted to £1,400.

(h)   She estimates that the cost of inventory of materials that she had left at the end of the year was £2,200.

Task 10.1

Calculate the total purchases for the year ended 30 September 20X3.

Task 10.2

Calculate the total cost of goods sold for the year ended 30 September 20X3.

Task 10.3

Calculate revenue for the year ended 30 September 20X3.

Task 10.4

Show the entries that would appear in Sheena Gordon's cash account.

Task 10.5

Calculate the total drawings made by Sheena Gordon throughout the year.

Task 10.6

Calculate the figure for net profit for the year ended 30 September 20X3.

 Test your understanding 11

Fariah is a sole trader running an IT support business and prepares accounts to 31 December 20X8. The summary of her bank account is as follows.

	£		£
Balance b/d 1 Jan 20X8	25,000	Advertising	10,000
Receipts from receivables	80,000	General expenses	8,000
		Rent	9,000
		Payments to suppliers	10,000
		Drawings	36,000
		Balance at 31 Dec 20X8	32,000
	105,000		**105,000**

Receivables at 1 January 20X8 were £20,000 and at 31 December 20X8 were £30,000, after accounting for the contra transaction explained below.

Payables at 1 January 20X8 were £13,000 and at 31 December 20X8 were £15,000, after accounting for the contra transaction explained below.

All Fariah's sales are on credit. One of Fariah's receivables has been made bankrupt owing her £3,400. She wrote this debt off in November 20X8.

Fariah offset an agreed amount of £300 with another business which makes both purchases and sales on credit to her.

During December 20X8 a payment of £3,000 was made for insurance which covered the period 1 November 20X8 to 31 October 20X9. Insurance is included in general expenses.

Fariah depreciated her computers at 40% reducing balance. The CV of the computers at 1 January 20X8 was £4,600.

Task 11.1

Calculate the capital at 1 January 20X8.

Task 11.2

Prepare the journal that Fariah would have made in November 20X8 to record the write off of the irrecoverable debt.

Journal

Account name	Dr (£)	Cr (£)
Narrative		

Task 11.3

Prepare the sales ledger control account for the year ended 31 December 20X8, showing credit sales as the balancing figure.

Sales ledger control account

	£		£

Task 11.4

Prepare the purchases ledger control account for the year ended 31 December 20X8, showing credit purchases as the balancing figure.

Purchases ledger control account

	£		£

Task 11.5

Prepare the general expenses account for the year ended 31 December 20X8.

General expenses account

	£		£

Task 11.6

Calculate the depreciation that Fariah will provide for the year ended 31 December 20X8.

Task 11.7

Prepare the journal that Fariah will make at the year end to record depreciation.

Account name	Dr (£)	Cr (£)
Narrative		

Task 11.8

Prepare a trial balance at 31 December 20X8. The trial balance should show the computers at their carrying amount (not cost less accumulated depreciation).

8 Summary

This chapter has covered all of the varying techniques that might be required to deal with an incomplete records problem in an examination.

The techniques are the net assets approach, cash and bank accounts, sales ledger control account and purchase ledger control account, plus use of mark-ups and margins.

Many of these questions will look formidable in an examination but they are all answerable if you think about all of these techniques that you have learnt and apply them to the particular circumstances of the question.

You will also find that the AAT style is to lead you through a question with small tasks prompting you to carry out the calculations in a particular order which makes the process more manageable.

Test your understanding answers

Test your understanding 1

Increase in net assets	=	capital introduced	+ profit – drawings
(17,300 – 14,600)	=	2,000	+ profit – 10,000
2,700	=	2,000	+ profit – 10,000
Profit	=	£10,700	

Test your understanding 2

Working cash account

	£		£
Balance b/d	50	Bankings	15,000
Capital (Bingo)	500	Wages	1,000
Cash sales (bal fig)	20,525	Expenses	5,000
		Balance c/d	75
	_____		_____
	21,075		21,075
	_____		_____

The rationale is that £21,075 has been 'used' for bankings, expenses and providing a float to start the next period therefore £21,075 must have been received.

Of this 'receipt':

- £50 is from last period; and

- £500 is an injection of capital.

Therefore £20,525 must have been sales.

Test your understanding 3

		%	£
(a)	Cost of goods sold	100	
	Add: mark–up	10	
	Therefore revenue	110	
	Therefore cost of goods sold	$^{100}/_{110}$ × £6,160	£5,600
(b)	Revenue	100	
	Less: gross profit	20	
	Therefore cost of goods sold	80	
	Therefore revenue	$^{100}/_{80}$ × £20,000	£25,000
(c)	Cost of goods sold	100	
	Add: mark–up	33	
	Therefore revenue	133	
	Therefore revenue	$^{133}/_{100}$ × £15,000	£19,950
(d)	Revenue	100	
	Less: gross profit	25	
	Therefore cost of goods sold	75	
	Therefore revenue	$^{100}/_{75}$ × £13,200	£17,600
(e)	Revenue	20,000	
	Less: cost of goods sold	16,000	
	Therefore gross profit	4,000	

Gross profit on revenue $\dfrac{4,000}{20,000} \times \dfrac{100}{1} = 20\%$

Gross profit on cost of goods sold $\dfrac{4,000}{16,000} \times \dfrac{100}{1} = 25\%$

KAPLAN PUBLISHING

Test your understanding 4

Task 1

Calculate the figure for purchases.

Purchase ledger control account

	£		£
Cash	9,000	Balance b/d	2,100
Balance c/d	2,600	Purchases (bal fig)	9,500
	11,600		11,600

Note that we are constructing the total account, and producing the balancing figure which represents the purchases made during the year.

Remember the double-entry involved here. The cash of £9,000 will be a credit in the cash account. The purchases (£9,500) will be debited to the purchases account and transferred to the statement of profit or loss at the year-end:

Purchases account

	£		£
Purchase ledger control account	9,500	Statement of P & L	9,500

Task 2

Now complete the cost of goods sold

	£
Opening inventory	1,800
Purchases	9,500
	11,300
Less: closing inventory	(1,600)
Cost of goods sold	9,700

Task 3

Now you can work out the cost structure and revenue.

(a) Work out the cost structure.

The mark-up is arrived at by reference to the cost of goods sold. Thus, cost of goods sold is 100%, the mark-up is 20% and therefore the revenues are 120%:

	%
Revenue (balancing figure)	120
Less: Gross profit	20
Cost of goods sold	100

(b) Revenue $= \dfrac{120}{100} \times$ cost of goods sold

$= \dfrac{120}{100} \times £9,700$

$= £11,640$

📝 Test your understanding 5

Task 1

Calculate purchases

Purchase ledger control account

	£		£
Cash – payments to suppliers	755	Payables 1/1/X4	3,845
Bank – payments to suppliers	59,660	Purchases (balancing figure)	61,225
Payables 31.12.X4	4,655		
	65,070		65,070

Task 2

Calculate the cost of goods sold.

	£
Opening inventory 1.1.X4	4,570
Purchases	61,225
	65,795
Inventory 31.12.X4	(5,375)
Cost of goods sold	60,420

Task 3

Calculate total sales

Cost of structure

Cost of goods sold = 100%

Mark-up   = $33^1/_3$%

Therefore sales   = $133^1/_3$%

$$\text{Sales} = \frac{\text{Cost of goods sold}}{100} \times 133^1/_3 = \frac{60,420}{100} \times 133^1/_3 = £80,560$$

Task 4

Calculate cash sales

	£
Total revenue	80,560
Less: credit sales (per question)	(12,760)
Therefore, cash sales	67,800

Task 5

Calculate drawings

Enter the cash sales in the cash account. This will give drawings as a balancing figure.

The cash account is reproduced here.

Cash account

	£		£
Balance 1.1.X4	12	Payments to suppliers	755
Receipts from cash sales	67,800	Other costs	155
		Wages	3,055
		Cash banked	59,000
		Drawings (balancing figure)	4,827
		Balance c/d	20
	67,812		67,812

Test your understanding 6

1. Increase in net assets = capital introduced + profit – drawings

2. Debit   Bank account
   Credit   Cash account

3. £17,500 + 1,500 – £1,000   =   £18,000

4. £12,200 + £1,200 – £800   =   £12,600

5. £2,000 × 120/100   =   £2,400

6. £2,000 × 100/80   =   £2,500

7. £24,000 × 75/100   =   £18,000

8. £24,000 × 100/125   =   £19,200

9. Cost of goods sold = £100,000 × 60/100   =   £60,000
   Opening inventory + purchases   =   £65,000
   Closing inventory   =   £5,000

10. Cost of goods sold = £80,000 × 100/125   =   £64,000
    Purchases = £64,000 + £8,000 – £10,000 =   £62,000

Test your understanding 7

(a) Sales for the year

Sales ledger control account

	£		£
01/6/X0 Balance b/d	2,000	31/5/X1 Discount allowed	2,750
31/5/X1 Sales (bal fig)	47,550	31/5/X1 Receipts (bank)	45,000
		31/5/X1 Balance c/d	1,800
	49,550		49,550

(b) Purchases for the year

Purchase ledger control account

	£		£
31/5/X1 Payments (bank)	36,200	01/6/X0 Balance b/d	1,200
31/5/X1 Purchase returns	1,280	31/5/X1 Purchases (bal fig)	37,780
31/5/X1 Balance c/d	1,500		
	38,980		38,980

(c) **Statement of profit or loss of Peter Ryan trading as 'Brew-By Us' for the year ended 31 May 20X1**

	£	£
Revenue		47,550
Inventory at 1 June 20X0	6,000	
Add Purchases	37,780	
Less Purchase returns	(1,280)	
	42,500	
Less Inventory 31 May 20X1	(8,000)	
Cost of goods sold		(34,500)
Gross profit		13,050
Expenses		
Wages	3,850	
Advertising	750	
Heat and light	1,060	
Insurance	400	
Rent and rates	5,200	
Bank charges	55	
Discount allowed	2,750	
Stationery	200	
Depreciation charge		
Fixtures (15% × £2,000)	300	
Total expenses		(14,565)
Loss for the year		(1,515)

Statement of financial position as at 31 May 20X1

	Cost £	Depreciation £	CV £
Non-current assets			
Fixtures and fittings	2,000	300	1,700
	2,000	300	1,700
Current assets			
Inventory		8,000	
Receivables		1,800	
		9,800	
Current liabilities			
Payables		1,500	
Bank overdraft		1,930	
		3,430	
Net current assets			6,370
Non-current liabilities			
Loan			4,000
Net assets			4,070
Capital		5,785	
Less Loss for year		(1,515)	
		4,270	
Less Drawings		(200)	
Proprietors funds			4,070

Test your understanding 8

(a)   Revenue for the year

Sales ledger control account

	£		£
01/6/X0 Balance b/d	16,000	31/5/X1 Bank	79,000
31/5/X1 Sales (bal fig)	83,100	31/5/X1 Discounts	1,100
		31/5/X1 Balance c/d	19,000
	99,100		99,100
01/6/X1 Balance b/d	19,000		

	£
Credit sales	83,100
Cash sales banked	7,700
Expenses paid by cash	420
Cash for personal use	15,600
Total revenue	106,820

(b)   Purchases for the year

Purchase ledger control account

	£		£
31/5/X1 Payments	70,000	01/6/X0 Balance b/d	15,000
31/5/X1 Discounts	1,800	31/5/X1 (Purchases) bal fig	76,800
31/5/X1 Balance c/d	20,000		
	91,800		91,800

(c)

Rates account

	£		£
01/6/X0 Balance b/d	1,200	31/5/X1 Profit or loss	3,800
31/5/X1 Payments	4,200	31/5/X1 Balance c/d	1,600
	5,400		5,400
01/6/X1 Balance b/d	1,600		

Telephone account

	£		£
31/5/X1 Payments	1,200	01/6/X0 Balance b/d	400
31/5/X1 Balance c/d	500	31/5/X1 Profit or loss	1,300
	1,700		1,700
		01/6/X1 Balance b/d	500

Heat and light

	£		£
31/5/X1 Payments	1,800	01/6/X0 Balance b/d	300
31/5/X1 Balance c/d	500	31/5/X1 Profit or loss	2,000
	2,300		2,300
		01/6/X1 Balance b/d	500

(d) Statement of profit or loss for year ended 31 May 20X1

	£	£
Revenue		106,820
Inventory – 1/6/X0	10,000	
Add: purchases	76,800	
	86,800	
Less: Inventory 31/5/X1	16,000	
Cost of goods sold		70,800
Gross profit		36,020
Discounts received		1,800
Expenses		
Heat and light	2,000	
Office expenses (2,600 + 420)	3,020	
Rent and rates	3,800	
Telephone	1,300	
Wages	9,800	
Vehicle expenses	1,200	
Insurance	800	
Depreciation charge		
Warehouse fittings	1,600	
Van	1,300	
Discounts allowed	1,100	
Total expenses		25,920
Profit for the year for year		11,900

Statement of financial position as at 31 May 20X1

	£	£
Non-current assets		
Warehouse fittings (8,000 – 1,600)		6,400
Van (6,500 – 1,300)		5,200
		11,600
Current assets		
Inventory	16,000	
Trade receivables	19,000	
Prepayment (rates)	1,600	
Cash at bank	900	
	37,500	
Current liabilities		
Trade payables	20,000	
Accruals (500 + 500)	1,000	
	21,000	
Net current assets		16,500
Net assets		28,100
Capital (W)		29,300
Add: capital introduced (caravan sale)		2,500
Add: profit for year		11,900
		43,700
Less: drawings		15,600
Proprietors funds		28,100

Working

The opening capital can be entered as the balancing figure on the statement of financial position. Alternatively it can be proved as follows:

	£
Fittings	8,000
Inventory	10,000
Receivables	16,000
Payables	(15,000)
Prepayments	1,200
Accruals	(700)
Bank	9,800
	29,300

Test your understanding 9

(a)

	£	%
Revenue	200,000	160
Cost of goods sold		100
Gross profit ($\frac{60}{160} \times 200,000$)	75,000	60

(b)

	£	%
Revenue = (($\frac{100}{70}$) × 210,000)	300,000	100
Cost of goods sold (see below)	210,000	70
Gross profit	90,000	30

Cost of goods sold	
Opening inventory	40,000
Purchases	180,000
Closing inventory	(10,000)
	210,000

Test your understanding 10

Task 10.1

Total purchases

	£
Purchase of inventory bought in October	1,800
Purchases (bank)	18,450
Cash payments	3,800
Closing payables	1,400
	25,450

Task 10.2

Cost of goods sold

	£
Purchases	25,450
Less closing inventory	2,200
	23,250

Task 10.3

Sales for the year

If GP margin on sales is 50% then sales are $£23,250 \times \dfrac{100}{50} = £46,500$

Task 10.4

Cash account			
	£		£
Cash sales	46,500	Bankings	27,000
		Materials	3,800
		General expenses	490
		Drawings (bal fig)	15,110
		Float balance c/d	100
	46,500		46,500

Task 10.5

	£
Cash drawings (from Task 4)	15,110
Bank	6,200
	————
	21,310
	————

Task 10.6

	£
Gross profit	23,250
Less expenses:	
General expenses (870 + 490)	(1,360)
Depreciation (4,000 × 1/5)	(800)
	————
Profit for the year	21,090
	————

Test your understanding 11

Task 11.1

Capital at 1 January 20X8

	£
Bank	25,000
Trade receivables	20,000
Computers	4,600
Trade payables	(13,000)
	————
Capital	36,600
	————

Tutorial note. Remember that capital equals net assets. You therefore have to list all the assets and liabilities at the start of the year to find the net assets and therefore the capital.

Task 11.2

Journal

Account name	Dr (£)	Cr (£)
Irrecoverable debt expense	3,400	
Sales ledger control account		3,400
Narrative	Being the irrecoverable debt	

Task 11.3

Sales ledger control account

	£		£
Balance b/d 1 Jan 20X8	20,000	Cash from receivables	80,000
		Irrecoverable debt	3,400
		Contra with PLCA	300
Credit sales (bal fig)	93,700	Balance c/d 31 Dec 20X8	30,000
	113,700		113,700

Task 11.4

Purchases ledger control account

	£		£
Paid to payables	10,000	Balance b/d 1 Jan 20X8	13,000
Contra with SLCA	300		
Balance c/d 31 Dec 20X8	15,000	Purchases (bal fig)	12,300
	25,300		25,300

Task 11.5

General expenses account

	£		£
Cash paid	8,000	Profit or loss	5,500
		Balance c/d	2,500
	8,000		8,000

Tutorial note. The insurance payment of £3,000 includes a prepayment of £3,000 × 10/12 = £2,500.

Task 11.6

Depreciation for the year ended 31 December 20X8

	£
CV at 1 January 20X8	4,600
Depreciation for the year at 40%	1,840
	————
	2,760
	————

Task 11.7

Journal

Account name	Dr (£)	Cr (£)
Depreciation expense	1,840	
Accumulated dep'n – computers		1,840
Narrative	Being the depreciation for the non-current assets for the year	

Task 11.8

Trial balance as at 31 December 20X8

	£	£
Capital at 1 October 20X7		36,600
Bank	32,000	
Sales		93,700
Sales ledger control a/c	30,000	
Purchases	12,300	
Purchases ledger control a/c		15,000
Advertising	10,000	
General expenses	5,500	
Prepayment – general expenses	2,500	
Rent	9,000	
Drawings	36,000	
Depreciation charge	1,840	
Irrecoverable debt expense	3,400	
Computers	2,760	
	————	————
	145,300	145,300

Financial reporting and ethical principles

Introduction

This chapter provides some essential background knowledge of the principles and concepts that underlie the preparation of financial statements for different types of organisation.

It also looks at the ethical principles that should be complied with when preparing final accounts.

ASSESSMENT CRITERIA	CONTENTS
Describe the types of organisation that need to prepare final accounts (1.1)	1 Introduction
Recognise the regulations applying to different types of organisation (1.2)	2 Different types of organisations which prepare final accounts
Describe the primary users of final accounts and their needs (2.1)	3 Differences between preparing sole trader accounts and limited company accounts
Describe the accounting principles underlying the preparation of final accounts (2.2)	4 Primary users of the accounts
Apply ethical principles when preparing final accounts (2.3)	5 The legal and regulatory framework
Describe the main sources of regulation governing company accounts (6.1)	6 The underlying assumptions
Describe the more detailed reporting arising from these regulations (6.2)	7 The qualitative characteristics
	8 Ethical principles when preparing final accounts

1 Introduction

1.1 Introduction

In this chapter we will be covering background information that is essential for your understanding of the preparation of financial statements for many types of organisation.

We will also review the fundamental code of ethics, published by The International Federation of Accountants (IFAC), which forms the basis for the ethical codes of many accountancy bodies, including the AAT, ICAEW, ACCA and CIMA.

2 Different types of organisations which prepare final accounts

2.1 For-profit organisations

For-profit organisations are businesses whose primary goal is earning a profit. Most businesses are for-profit organisations; for example retail stores, restaurants, supermarkets and insurance companies.

2.2 Not-for-profit organisations

Not-for-profit organisations are types of organisation that do not earn profits for their owners or stakeholders. All of the money earned by or donated to a not-for-profit organisation is used in pursuing the organisation's objectives.

They are usually charities or other types of public service organisation; this may include; Housing Associations, the Financial Ombudsman, Sports and Social Clubs and some charity backed Hospices.

2.3 Sole traders

Sole traders are businesses which are owned and managed by one individual. There is no legal distinction between the owner and the business. The owner is responsible for any business debts e.g. if the business bank account had an overdraft.

2.4 Partnerships

A partnership is two or more people carrying on business together with a view to making a profit and sharing that profit. The partners both own and manage the business. If the partnership makes a loss shown in their statement of profit or loss then this will need to be shared between the partners in the same way that profits are shared. In a similar way to a sole trader, the partners are collectively responsible for any business debts.

Some advantages and disadvantages of operating as a partnership rather than a sole trader are shown below:

Advantages	Disadvantages
Availability of funds – The partners will fund the business with start-up capital. This means that the more partners there are, the more money they can put into the business, which will allow more potential for growth.	**Partnership agreement** – partners must decide on how they are going to share profits and set up their partnership agreement.
Responsibility – Partners can share the responsibility of the running of the business. This will allow them to make the most of their individual skills and abilities. So if one partner is good with figures, they might deal with the book keeping and accounts, while the other partner might have experience in sales and therefore be the main sales person for the business.	**Disagreements** – People are likely to have different ideas on how the business should be run, who should be doing what and what the best interests of the business are. This can lead to disagreements and disputes which might not only harm the business, but also the relationship of those involved.
Making decisions – Partners share the decision making and can help each other out when they need to. More partners means more business ideas and help for solving of problems that the business encounters.	**Tax and apportioning profits** – Each partner needs to submit their own self-assessment tax return after their share of the profits has been distributed and their taxable profit has been calculated. A sole trader does not need to distribute the profit because there is only one owner.

Test your understanding 1

Which of the following is an advantage of operating as a sole trader rather than a partnership?

- Sole traders do not have to submit a tax return.

- Sole traders can make their own decisions regarding the running of their business without having to consult others.

- Partnerships have more than one owner so usually more funds are available to be invested in the business as capital.

- Sole trader businesses have to prepare their accounts in accordance with the relevant accounting standards.

2.5 Limited companies

Limited companies are classed as a legal entity in its own right where the shareholders (investors) are the owners. Limited companies are 'limited by shares'. This means that the shareholders' responsibility for the company's financial liabilities is limited to the value of shares that they own but haven't yet paid for.

Directors are responsible for running the company. Directors often own shares. Company directors are not personally responsible for debts the company can't pay if the business gets into financial difficulties.

2.6 Limited liability partnerships

Limited liability partnerships (LLPs) are partnerships where some of the partners have limited liability similar to shareholders in a company as mentioned above. There must be at least one partner with unlimited liability. This differs from a sole trader business where the owner is personally liable for the business debts. Unlike shareholders in a limited company, the partners have the right to manage the business directly.

2.7 Charities

To be classed as a charity, an organisation must meet the definition of a charity set out in the Charities Act 2011. It must be established for charitable purposes only, meaning that it must be for the general benefit of the public. It needs to be established for specific purposes for example the advancement of education, the advancement of religion and the advancement of arts and culture.

3 Differences between preparing sole trader accounts and limited company accounts

3.1 Introduction

In this section we look at some key differences between the final accounts of a sole trader or a partnership business compared to the final accounts of a limited company.

3.2 Table of some key differences

Sole traders/Partnerships	Limited Company
Sole traders/partners both own and manage the business.	The company is a separate legal entity. The shareholders are the owners and investors of the business and the directors run the company on behalf of the shareholders.
Sole traders/partners are not legally required to produce annual accounts or file accounts for inspection. However, a record of business expenses and personal income are required for tax returns.	A limited company must prepare annual accounts (also known as 'statutory accounts') from the company's records at the end of the financial year. The annual accounts should be accompanied by notes to the accounts which include accounting policies adopted by the company, a breakdown of the receivables balance, and how the carrying amount of each type of asset has been calculated. These are to be filed with HMRC as part of its tax return as well as sent to all shareholders and Companies House. Accounts must be prepared in line with accounting standards.
Tax does not appear in a sole trader's statement of profit or loss i.e. it is not a business expense. For a partnership each partner must prepare a separate self-assessment tax return but it is still not classed as a business expense in the same way as a sole trader.	Limited companies pay tax, and this will be charged to the statement of profit or loss as an expense. The tax will not be paid until after the year-end, and so the charge for the year will be a liability at the year-end. The closing liability is an estimate, and any over-estimate or under-estimate is reversed out through the following year's statement of profit or loss.

A sole trader can take drawings from the business for personal expenses. These drawings are added back to the profits when calculating the taxable profits for the business.	Dividends for limited companies are the equivalent of drawings for a sole trader. Dividends are reported in the statement of changes in equity.

3.3 Advantages and disadvantages of incorporated status

There are certain advantages and disadvantages associated with trading as a company rather than as a sole trader.

The advantages are as follows:

- If a company goes into liquidation the owners of the company (the shareholders) are only liable to pay any amounts that they have not yet paid for the shares that they hold. A sole trader would be personally liable for any outstanding debts of the business.

- The shareholders can share in the profits of the business without necessarily having to work day-to-day for the business.

- Companies are in a better position when borrowing money; for example they can issue debentures.

- The company will continue in existence even if shareholders die. If a sole trader dies the business will only continue if the business is sold. This is known as 'perpetual succession'.

The disadvantages are as follows:

- A large company (i.e. one that meets certain size criteria) must normally have an audit of its accounts and therefore must pay auditors' fees. However an audit also offers benefits to the company.

- A company must prepare its accounts in a format prescribed by legislation.

- A company suffers a greater administrative burden than a sole trader. For example, it must file its accounts each year with the Registrar of Companies and must hold an Annual General Meeting of its shareholders.

4 Primary users of the accounts

4.1 Introduction

The main purpose of financial statements is to provide information to a wide range of users. However, many different groups of people may use financial statements and each group will need particular information for different reasons.

4.2 Primary users of the accounts

User	Needs
Investors	Investors need to be able to assess the ability of a business to pay dividends and manage resources.
Lenders	Lenders such as banks are interested in the ability of the business to pay interest and repay loans.
Other creditors	To decide whether to supply goods on credit and the terms of the credit.

5 The legal and regulatory framework

5.1 Introduction

The regulatory framework for a UK company preparing financial statements in accordance with international standards consists of:

- The Companies Act 2006 which applies to all UK companies regardless of whether they follow UK or international accounting rules

- The International Accounting Standards Board and its associated bodies who are responsible for the setting of International Financial Reporting Standards (IFRSs).

An entity adopts the accounting policies most appropriate to its particular circumstances for the purpose of giving a true and fair view;

Limited liability partnerships (LLPs) are hybrids between a partnership and a limited company formed under the Limited Liability Partnerships Act 2000. Many of the provisions of the Companies Act 2006 also apply to LLPs.

The presentation of final accounts for sole trader and partnership businesses are not governed by the statue and accounting regulations to the same extent those for limited companies or LLPs are; they have no definitive format, but normally follow the principles of limited company accounts as good practice.

5.2   IFRSs and IASs

Accounting standards give guidance in specific areas of accounting. The syllabus for this unit applies international standards which consist of the following:

- *International Financial Reporting Standards (IFRSs)*

  These are issued by the International Accounting Standards Board. Many countries have used IFRSs for some years. In 2002, the Council of Ministers of the European Union (EU) decided that any company which is listed on a European Stock Exchange must prepare their consolidated accounts in line with IFRSs with effect from 1 January 2005.

- *International Accounting Standards (IASs)*

  IASs were created by the International Accounting Standards Committee (IASC) the predecessor of the IASB. When the IASB was formed it adopted the standards of the IASC which were called IASs. In recent times, the IASB has introduced many new standards so several IASs have now been superseded.

- *IAS 1 Presentation of the Financial Statements*

  This accounting standard sets out the overall requirements for financial statements for organisations adopting IFRSs, including how they should be structured, the minimum requirements for their content and overriding concepts such as going concern, the accruals basis of accounting and the format and classification of financial statements. The standard requires a complete set of financial statements to comprise a statement of financial position, a statement of profit or loss and other comprehensive income, a statement of changes in equity and a statement of cash flows. You will see the format of the statement of changes in equity and statement of cash flows later on in your AAT studies.

- *IAS 2 Inventories*

  This accounting standard contains the requirements on how to account for most types of inventory. The standard requires inventories to be measured at the lower of cost and net realisable value (NRV).

- *IAS 16 Property, Plant and Equipment*

  This accounting standard outlines the accounting treatment for most types of property, plant and equipment. Property, plant and equipment is measured at its cost and depreciated so that its depreciable amount is allocated over its useful economic life.

5.3 Charity legislation

All charities prepare accounts on an accruals basis. They must prepare a statement of financial position at the end of each reporting period.

The statement of financial position provides a snapshot of a charity's assets and liabilities (net assets) and how these are represented by the different classes of funds held by a charity.

The objective of the statement of financial position is to show the resources available to the charity and whether these are available for all purposes of the charity or have to be used for specific purposes.

The Charity Commission for England and Wales and the Office of the Scottish Charity Regulator make up the joint SORP (Statements of Recommended Practice)-making body. The charities SORP gives guidance on financial accounting and reporting for charitable entities. The Charity Commission and the Office of the Scottish Charities Regulator are responsible for issuing the Statement of Recommended Practice (SORP) for charities.

Charities don't pay tax on most types of income as long as they use the money for charitable purposes.

 Test your understanding 2

State whether the following are true or false.

- Sole trader businesses have to prepare their accounts in accordance with the relevant accounting standards

- IAS 2 states that inventories should be valued at the greater of cost and net realisable value.

- Charities must satisfy the definition of a charity which is outlined in the Charities Act.

- For a company, the directors always manage operations and own the company.

---

6 The underlying assumptions

6.1 Introduction

The underlying assumptions governing the financial statements are:

- going concern
- accruals.

6.2 Going concern

The going concern basis assumes that the entity will continue in operation for the foreseeable future and has neither the need nor the intention to liquidate or curtail materially the scale of its operations.

If the business is no longer considered to be a going concern, the assets of the business would need to be recognised at the amount which is expected from their sale. Liabilities would be recognised at the amounts that are likely to be settled.

6.3 Accruals basis:

The accruals basis states that transactions should be reflected in the financial statements for the period in which they occur. This means that income should be recognised as it is earned and expenses when they are incurred, rather than when cash is received or paid.

Test your understanding 3

One of your clients, Olivia Ryan, has been making quite substantial losses for the last 6 years, which accounting concept is relevant to preparing the accounts for this client?

- None
- Going concern
- Accruals
- Prudence

---

7 The qualitative characteristics

7.1 Introduction

The Conceptual Framework for Financial Reporting identifies two fundamental qualitative characteristics of useful financial information:

- relevance, and
- faithful representation.

These are supported by four enhancing qualitative characteristics:

- comparability
- verifiability
- timeliness, and
- understandability

7.2 Definitions

 Definitions

Relevance
Financial information is regarded as relevant if it is capable of influencing the decisions of users.

Faithful representation
This means that financial information must be complete, neutral and free from error.

Comparability
It should be possible to compare an entity over time and with similar information about other entities.

Verifiability
If information can be verified (e.g. through an audit) this provides assurance to the users that it is both credible and reliable.

Timeliness
Information should be provided to users within a timescale suitable for their decision-making purposes.

Understandability
Information should be understandable to those who may want to review and use it. This can be facilitated through appropriate classification, characterisation and presentation of information.

8 Ethical principles when preparing final accounts

8.1 Introduction

In this section we review the Code of Ethics for Professional Accountants relating to the preparation of final accounts.

8.2 The Code of Ethics for Professional Accountants

The Code of Ethics for Professional Accountants, published by The International Federation of Accountants (IFAC), forms the basis for the ethical codes of many accountancy bodies, including the AAT, ICAEW, ACCA and CIMA.

The Code adopts a principles-based approach. It does not attempt to cover every situation where a member may encounter professional ethical issues, prescribing the way in which he or she should respond. Instead, it adopts a value system, focusing on fundamental professional and ethical principles which are at the heart of proper professional behaviour.

The five key principles are as follows:

(a) Integrity

A person should be straightforward and honest in performing professional work and in all business relationships.

(b) Objectivity

A professional accountant should not allow bias, conflict of interest or undue influence of others to override professional or business judgments.

(c) Professional competence and due care

A professional accountant has a continuing duty to maintain professional knowledge and skill at the level required to ensure that a client or employer receives competent professional service based on current developments in practice, legislation and techniques.

(d) Confidentiality

A professional accountant should respect the confidentiality of information acquired as a result of professional and business relationships and should not disclose any such information to third parties without proper and specific authority unless there is a legal or professional right or duty to disclose.

Test your understanding 4

During your lunch you read an article in the FT about a case where a company was prosecuted through the courts for a breach of environmental laws regarding the dumping of toxic waste into drains, which subsequently lead to the open ocean. The case included testimony from the company's auditors which secured the prosecution.

You discussed this with one of the juniors who said that she thought that this would constitute a breach of confidentiality on behalf of the auditor. Explain why this is not the case.

(e)   Professional behaviour

A person should not act in any way that is unprofessional or does not comply with relevant laws and regulations.

8.3   Threats

Threats to compliance with the fundamental principles can be general in nature or relate to the specific circumstances of an appointment.

General categories of threats to the principles include the following:

- **The self-interest threat** – a threat to a member's integrity or objectivity   may stem from a financial or other self-interest conflict.

  This could arise, for example, from a direct or indirect interest in a client or from fear of losing an engagement or having his or her employment terminated.

- **The self-review threat** – there will be a threat to objectivity if any product or judgement made by the member or the firm needs to be challenged or re-evaluated by him or her subsequently i.e. can you effectively review your own work?

- **The advocacy threat** – there is a threat to a member's objectivity if he or she becomes an advocate for or against the position taken by the client or employer in any adversarial proceedings or situation. The degree to which this presents a threat to objectivity will depend on the individual circumstances. The presentation of only one side of the case may be compatible with objectivity provided that it is accurate and truthful.

- **The familiarity or trust threat** – is a threat that the member may become influenced by his or her

    - knowledge of the issue

    - relationship with the client or employer

    - judgement of the qualities of the client or employer to the extent that he or she becomes too trusting.

- **The intimidation threat** – the possibility that the member may become intimidated by threat, by a dominating personality, or by other pressures, actual or feared, applied by the client or employer or by another.

 Test your understanding 5

Consider each of the following threats to independence and label them according to the nature of the ethical threat.

- The financial statements of Hird Ltd have been prepared by Lloyd Brothers, their audit firm.

- Having audited the client company for many years, the audit partner has become close friends with the company directors.

- Knowalot plc has intimated to the audit company that if they do not receive an unqualified audit report for the year 20X9, they may put the audit out to tender next year.

---

9 Summary

The presentation of final accounts for sole trader and partnership businesses are not governed by the statue and accounting regulations to the same extent as those for limited companies and LLPs.

The primary users of the accounts are investors, lenders and other creditors who all have different needs for using final accounts.

The regulatory framework for a UK company preparing final accounts under international standards consists of: The Companies Act and The International Accounting Standards Board and its associated bodies.

The Framework for the Preparation and Presentation of Financial Statements sets out two fundamental accounting concepts; going concern and accruals. The two fundamental qualitative characteristics of financial information are: relevance and faithful representation and the four enhancing qualitative characteristics of financial information are: comparability, verifiability, timeliness and understandability.

The five key principles which make up the code of ethics are: integrity, objectivity, professional competence, confidentiality and professional behaviour.

Test your understanding answers

Test your understanding 1

Sole traders can make their own decisions regarding the running of their business without having to consult others.

Test your understanding 2

- **False** – the presentation of sole trader and partnership accounts are not governed by the same accounting regulations as limited company accounts.

- **False** – inventories should be valued at the lower of cost and net realisable value

- **True**

- **False** – directors manage operations but the shareholders (investors) are the owners.

Test your understanding 3

Going concern is the relevant accounting concept here as there is doubt over whether the business will continue trading for the foreseeable future.

Test your understanding 4

Accountants have a duty of confidentiality.

However, there are occasions where the accountant has a professional or legal duty to disclose the information and therefore the breach of confidentiality is permissible.

Environmental damage is one such instance.

Test your understanding 5

- Self-review – the audit company cannot effectively review their own work.

- Familiarity – the audit partners may be influenced by their close relationship with the company directors.

- Intimidation – The audit company may become intimidated by Knowalot plc's threat to seek the services of an alternative audit company.

MOCK ASSESSMENT AQ2016

1 Mock Assessment Questions AQ2016

Task 1 (15 marks)

You are working on the final accounts of a business with a year-end of 31 March 2010. Currently the business does not use a double-entry system so you are to prepare the ledger accounts for SLCA, sales tax and bank for the first time. You have the following information:

Balances	
Account	**Year-end 31/03/09**
	£
SLCA	292,886
PLCA	267,900
Sales tax owed to HMRC	32,977
Bank overdraft	485

Details for year-ended 31 March 2010

- Credit sales were £422,875 plus sales tax.

- Credit purchases were £303,384 inclusive of sales tax.

- Cash sales were £109,122 including sales tax.

- Receipts from receivables were £452,080.

- Payments to payables were £298,456.

- A contra was processed at the value of £9,800.

- The business purchased a motor car costing £31,000 plus sales tax, and paid for it with a cheque.

- Office Expenses amounted to £590 exclusive of sales tax and were paid from the bank.

- The sales tax owed at 31/03/09 was paid to HMRC.

- Wages were paid that totalled £28,820.

- Closing balances for receivables and payables were £318,422 and £341,221 respectively.

- Assume a sales tax rate of 20%.

(a) Using the figures given above, prepare the sales ledger control account for year-ended 31 March 2010. Show clearly discounts as the balancing figure. Your answers should be shown to the nearest whole £ (4 marks)

SLCA

Date	Details	Amount £	Date	Details	Amount £

(b) Using the figures above, prepare the sales tax account for year-ended 31 March 2010. Show clearly the carried down figure. Your answers should be shown to the nearest whole £ (5 marks)

Sales tax

Date	Details	Amount £	Date	Details	Amount £

(c)   Using the figures above, prepare the bank account for year-ended 31 March 2010. Show clearly the carried down figure.

(6 marks)

Bank

Date	Details	Amount £	Date	Details	Amount £

Task 2   (15 marks)

This is a task about calculating missing balances.

A sales margin of 30% applies to the business.

Sales in the period amounted to £356,460.

Purchases amounted to £213,699.

Closing inventory amounted to £45,378.

(a)   Draw up the trading account clearly showing the figure for opening inventory.   (5 marks)

Trading account	£	£

(b) The trader has decided to introduce credit terms and allow customers to settle their account up to 30 days after purchase. What is the most likely figure outstanding on the trade receivables account at the year end?   (2 marks)

£358,000   ☐

£356,460   ☐

£0   ☐

£128,210   ☐

(c) Another trader's assets and liabilities are shown in the table below. Using the information in the table below calculate the capital invested during the year. At the start of the year the balance on the capital account was £43,000. Show your answer in the box below.   (3 marks)

	£
Motor vehicles	130,000
Inventory	45,760
Receivables	97,447
Bank (credit balance on bank statement)	11,978
Payables	65,398
Loan	20,000
Capital	?
Profit	148,677
Drawings	6,890

£ _____

(d) **Tick the boxes to show what effect this transaction will have on the balances:** (4 marks)

A trader makes drawings of goods during the year.

Account name	Debit ✓	Credit ✓	No change ✓
Bank			
Purchases			
Drawings			
Revenue			

(e) **You are working on the accounts of another client. Your manager has asked you to prepare the client's statement of profit or loss while he is out of the office but you have not yet had any training for this. Which one of the five key ethical principles is relevant here?** (1 mark)

Integrity / Objectivity / Professional competence and due care / Confidentiality / Professional behaviour

Task 3 (18 marks)

This task is about final accounts for sole traders.

You have been asked to assist in the preparation of the accounts for Prassas Trading for the year-ending 31 March 2011

Trial balance as at 31 March 2011		
	Dr	Cr
	£	£
Accruals		366
Administration expenses	23,245	
Allowance for doubtful debts		1,300
Bank		755
Capital		210,000
Cash	2,373	
Closing inventory	2,170	2,170
Drawings	1,500	
Depreciation charge	7,100	
Equipment cost	290,500	
Equipment accumulated depreciation		56,690
Heat, light and gas	7,200	
Prepayments	2,120	
Rent received		19,910
Loan		28,000
Opening inventory	2,350	
PLCA		52,342
Purchases	314,577	
Rent	9,000	
Revenue		544,512
SLCA	157,200	
Sales tax		5,390
Wages	102,100	
	921,435	921,435

- The statement of profit or loss has already been prepared and shows a profit for the year of £101,020.

- Prassas Trading has a policy of showing trade receivables net of any allowance for doubtful debts.

(a) **Using the information above, calculate the value of the net trade receivables to be shown in the statement of financial position.**

£ [   ]   (2 marks)

(b) **Prepare the statement of financial position for Prassas Trading as at 31 March 2011**   (16 marks)

	£	£	£
Non-current assets			
Current assets			
Current liabilities			
Net current assets			
Non-current liabilities			
Net assets			
Capital			

Task 4 (16 marks)

(a) (10 marks)

(i) **Which of the following is an advantage of running a business as a partnership over a limited company? Underline the correct answer.**

Limited liability / Full control over business decision making / The business is a separate legal entity / The shareholders are the owners

(ii) **Which of the following statements are true? You can tick more than one box.**

Charities need to be established for specific purposes. ☐

Charities do not need to prepare a statement of financial position at the end of each reporting period. ☐

To be classed as a charity, an organisation must meet the definition of a charity set out in the Charities Act. ☐

(iii) **Which of the following businesses have owners with limited liability? You can tick more than one box.**

1 Hightopp Ltd ☐

2 Hightopp LLP ☐

3 Lee & High Partnership ☐

(b) **Which of the following requires inventory to be valued at the lower of cost and net realisable value (NRV)?** (2 marks)

IAS 1 ☐

IAS 2016 ☐

IAS 2 ☐

(c) **Link the users of final accounts on the left below with the most likely reason for their interest on the right.** (4 marks)

Making decisions regarding their investment

Trade Payables	To assess the security of any loan

Shareholders	To compare to information from other organisations operating in the same sector

To decide whether to continue supplying goods on credit

Task 5 (15 marks)

Task 5 and Task 6 are about final accounts for a partnership. The information below is required for both tasks.

General information

- The profit sharing ratio is as follows:

  Brett – 40%

  Matt – 20%

  Bernard – 40%

- Bernard left the partnership on 31 March 2010. Goodwill was valued at £250,000 on this date.

- Brett and Matt will share profits in the ratio 3:1 from 1 April 2010.

- Brett and Bernard were awarded salaries during the year based on the work that they performed. The salaries were £8,000 and £6,000, respectively. The profit for the period is £24,920. Details of the interest on capital values are given below;

  Brett – £3,200 per annum

  Matt – £1,600 per annum

  Bernard – £2,000 per annum

- Bernard had a balance of £50,000 on his capital account from the beginning of the year until he left the partnership at the end of the accounting period.

Trial balance as at 31 March 2010		
	Dr	Cr
	£	£
Accruals		452
Administration expenses	35,879	
Allowance for doubtful debts		1,300
Allowance for doubtful debts adjustment		344
Bank		198
Capital – Brett		80,000
Capital – Matt		40,000
Cash	5,800	
Closing inventory	2,350	2,350
Current – Brett	1,340	
Current – Matt		4,120
Depreciation charge	9,990	
Discounts received		422
Disposal	4,300	
Equipment cost	227,000	
Equipment accumulated depreciation		46,700
Heat, light and gas	6,670	
Loan		34,000
Opening inventory	3,700	
PLCA		95,630
Prepayment	2,000	
Purchases	296,789	
Purchase returns		2,346
Rent	8,000	
Revenue		475,632
Sales returns	1,646	
SLCA	103,450	
Sales tax		14,620
Wages	89,200	
	798,114	798,114

(a) You need to prepare the appropriation account for the partnership for the year-ended 31 March 2010. Please do not use minus signs or brackets. (8 marks)

	£
Profit for appropriation	
Salaries:	
Interest on capital	
Residual profit or loss available for distribution	
Share of residual profit or loss:	

(b) Complete Bernard's capital account to deal with his retirement on 31 March 2010. It has been agreed that £10,000 will be paid straight to him and the remainder set up as a loan to the partnership. (2 marks)

Further information:

The **final balance** on Bernard's current account was £3,660 (credit)

CAPITAL – BERNARD

Date	Details	Amount £	Date	Details	Amount £

(c) Complete the goodwill account to deal with Bernard leaving the partnership on 1 November 2010. (5 marks)

GOODWILL

Date	Details	Amount £	Date	Details	Amount £

Task 6 (21 marks)

(a) Prepare the statement of profit or loss for the partnership for the year-ended 31 March 2010 based on the trial balance above. All year-end adjustments have been made. The only values to be shown as negatives should be a deduction from cost of sales and, if applicable, a net loss for the year. (14 marks)

	£	£
Revenue		
Cost of sales		
Gross profit		
Sundry income		
Total sundry income		
Expenses		
Total expenses		
Profit/(loss) for the year		

(b) **Calculate Brett's share of the profit or loss for the year and his closing current account balance.** (3 marks)

	£
Brett – share of profit or loss	
Brett – closing current account balance	

(c) **Where will the capital account balance for Brett appear on the statement of financial position?** (1 mark)

As a current asset. ☐

Within the 'Financed by' section. ☐

His capital account will not appear in the statement of financial position. ☐

(d) **Preparation of the final accounts for a limited company requires more detailed reporting than for a sole trader or a partnership.** (3 marks)

Which of the following statements is not correct for a limited company?

1   They have to prepare the accounts in line with accounting standards ☐

2   The taxation charge should be shown in the statement of profit or loss. ☐

3   Limited company accounts do not need to be prepared in a set format. ☐

1 Mock Assessment Answers AQ2016

Task 1 **(15 marks)**

(a) **(4 marks)**

SLCA

Date	Details	Amount £	Date	Details	Amount £
1/04/09	Bal b/d	292,886	31/03/10	Bank	452,080
31/03/10	Sales	507,450		Contra	9,800
				Discounts	**20,034**
				Bal c/d	318,422
		800,336			800,336

Credit sales = £422,875 plus 20% sales tax = £507,450

(b) **(5 marks)**

Sales tax

Date	Details	Amount £	Date	Details	Amount £
31/03/10	Purchases	50,564	1/04/09	Bal b/d	32,977
31/03/10	Office exp.	118	31/03/10	Credit sales	84,575
31/03/10	Bank	32,977	31/03/10	Cash sales	18,187
31/03/10	Discounts	3,339			
	Bal c/d	52,080			
		135,739			135,739

Sales tax on purchases = £303,384 × 20/120 = £50,564

Sales tax on office expenses = £590 × 20% = £118

Sales tax on discounts = £20,034 × 20/120 = £3,339

Sales tax on credit sales = £422,875 × 20% = £84,575

Sales tax on cash sales = £109,122 × 20/120 = £18,187

Sales tax on the car is not recoverable.

(c)   (6 marks)

Bank

Date	Details	Amount £	Date	Details	Amount £
31/03/10	Sales	109,122	01/04/09	Bal b/d	485
31/03/10	SLCA	452,080	31/03/10	PLCA	298,456
			31/03/10	Motor vehicles	37,200
			31/03/10	Office exps	708
			31/03/10	Sales tax	32,977
			31/03/10	Wages	28,820
				Bal c/d	162,556
		561,202			561,202

Motor vehicle cost = £31,000 plus 20% sales tax = £37,200.

Office expenses = £590 plus 20% sales tax = £708

Task 2   (15 marks)

(a)   (5 marks)

Trading account	£	£	%
Revenue		356,460	100
Opening inventory (bal. fig.)	81,201		
Purchases	213,699		
Closing inventory	(45,378)		
Cost of sales (356,460 × 70/100)		249,522	70
Gross profit (356,460 × 30/100)		106,938	30

(b)

£358,000	☐	(2 marks)
£356,460	☐	
£0	☐	
£128,210	✓	

(c) (3 marks)

	£
Opening capital	43,000
Capital introduced (answer)	**15,000**
Add profit	148,677
Less drawings	6,890
	————
Net assets (see workings below)	199,787
	————

Assets £130,000 + £45,760 + £97,447 + £11,978 = £285,185

Liabilities £65,398 + £20,000 = £85,398

Net assets £285,185 – £85,398 = £199,787

(d) (4 marks)

Account name	Debit ✓	Credit ✓	No change ✓
Bank			✓
Purchases		✓	
Drawings	✓		
Revenue			✓

(e) Professional competence and due care (1 mark)

Task 3 (18 marks)

(a) (2 marks)

£155,900

Working:

SLCA	£157,200
Allowance for doubtful debts	(£1,300)
Receivables	£155,900

(b) Statement of financial position for Prassas Trading as at 31 March 2011 (16 marks)

	£	£	£
Non-current assets			
Equipment	290,500	56,690	233,810
Current assets			
Inventory		2,170	
Receivables (a)		155,900	
Prepayments		2,120	
Cash		2,373	
		162,563	
Current liabilities			
Accruals	366		
Bank	755		
Payables	52,342		
Sales tax	5,390		
		58,853	
Net current assets			103,710
Non-current liabilities			
Loan			28,000
Net assets			**309,520**
Capital			
Opening capital			210,000
Add: Profit			101,020
Less: Drawings			1,500
Closing capital			309,520

Task 4 (16 marks)

(a) (10 marks)

(i) Full control over business decision making

(ii) Charities need to be established for specific purposes. ☑

Charities do not need to prepare a statement of financial position at the end of each reporting period. ☐

To be classed as a charity, an organisation must meet the definition of a charity set out in the Charities Act. ☑

(iii) 1 Hightopp Ltd ☑

2 Hightopp LLP ☑

3 Lee & High Partnership ☐

(b) (2 marks)

IAS 1 ☐

IAS 2016 ☐

IAS 2 ☑

(c) (4 marks)

Trade Payables	→	Making decisions regarding their investment
		To assess the security of any loan
Shareholders		To compare to information from other organisations operating in the same sector
	→	To decide whether to continue supplying goods on credit

Task 5 (15 marks)

(a) Prepare the appropriation account (8 marks)

	£
Profit for appropriation	24,920
Salaries:	
Brett	8,000
Bernard	6,000
Interest on capital	
Brett	3,200
Matt	1,600
Bernard	2,000
Residual profit or loss available for distribution	4,120
Share of residual profit or loss:	
Brett (40% × £4,120)	1,648
Matt (20% × £4,120)	824
Bernard (40% × £4,120)	1,648

(b) Prepare Bernard's capital account (2 marks)

CAPITAL – BERNARD

Date	Details	Amount £	Date	Details	Amount £
31/03/10	Bank	10,000	1/04/09	Bal b/d	50,000
31/03/10	Loan	143,660	31/03/10	Current a/c	3,660
			31/03/10	Goodwill	100,000
		153,660			153,660

(c) Complete the goodwill account   (5 marks)

GOODWILL

Date	Details	Amount £	Date	Details	Amount £
31/03/10	Capital – Brett (40%)	100,000	31/03/10	Capital – Brett (3/4)	187,500
	Capital – Matt (20%)	50,000		Capital – Matt (1/4)	62,500
	Capital – Bernard (40%)	100,000			
		250,000			250,000

Task 6   (21 marks)

(a) **Statement of profit or loss for the partnership for the year-ended 31 March 2010.**   (14 marks)

	£	£
Revenue (W1)		473,986
Cost of sales		
Opening inventory	3,700	
Purchases (W2)	294,443	
Closing inventory	(2,350)	
		295,793
Gross profit		**178,193**
Sundry income		
Allowance for doubtful debts adjustment		344
Discount received		422
Total sundry income		**766**

Expenses		
Administration expenses	35,879	
Depreciation charge	9,990	
Disposal	4,300	
Heat, light and gas	6,670	
Rent	8,000	
Wages	89,200	
Total expenses		**154,039**
Profit for the year		**24,920**

(W1) £475,632 – £1,646 = £473,986

(W2) £296,789 – £2,346 = £294,443

(b)   (3 marks)

	£
Brett – share of profit (from part 5(a) £8,000 + £3,200 + £1,648)	12,848
Brett – closing current account balance (£–1,340 + £12,848)	11,508

(c)   (1 mark)

As a current asset.   ☐

Within the 'Financed by' section.   ☑

His capital account will not appear in the statement of
financial position.   ☐

(d)   (3 marks)

1   They have to prepare the accounts in line with accounting
    standards   ☐

2   The taxation charge should be shown in the statement of
    profit or loss.   ☐

3   Limited company accounts do not need to be prepared
    in a set format.   ☑

INDEX